SENIOR READERS' THEATER

SENIOR READERS' THEATER

Humorous Skits for Senior Readers' Theater

JEAN MOSBY

CAUTION:

Professional and amateurs are hereby advised and warned that *Senior Readers' Theater* by Jean Mosby, being fully protected under the copyright laws of the U.S. and all other countries of the copyright union, is subject to royalties.

Copying from this book in whole or in part is forbidden by law and the right of performance is not implied. All rights, including professional and amateur production, recitation and public reading, are reserved.

These rights are controlled by author Jean Mosby.
Performance rights and permission to copy cast scripts may be requested per the Royalty Payment Form included in this book.

COVER PHOTOGRAPH - LARRY LINTON

PALMETTO
PUBLISHING

Charleston, SC
www.PalmettoPublishing.com

Senior Readers' Theater

Copyright © 2022 by Jean Mosby

All rights reserved.

No portion of this book may be reproduced, stored in a retrieval system, or transmitted in any form by any means– electronic, mechanical, photocopy, recording, or other–except for brief quotations in printed reviews, without prior permission of the author.

First Edition

Paperback ISBN: 979-8-8229-0542-9
ebook ISBN: 979-8-8229-0543-6

Table of Contents

A WEEKEND IN THE COUNTRY   1

A couple invites their new neighbors to go on a weekend retreat with them but the car ride proves them to be incompatible and the resort is not what they expected. Cast includes two men and three women. Runs seven minutes.

THE MARRIAGE ENRICHMENT COUNSELING SESSION   10

A couple seeks help from a marriage counselor, not because they have a bad marriage, but because they hope to "enrich" their marriage. The ensuing session provides laughs as they discuss their fifty years together. Cast includes a man, a woman, and a counselor who could be man or woman but is probably a woman. Runs ten minutes.

THE INCOME TAX AUDIT   22

A couple who run a small business cheat on their income tax return and are called to the IRS office for an audit. Their tax preparer has asked them to let her handle the audit alone, but they ignore her advice and show up anyway. She becomes increasingly frustrated as both husband and wife reveal far too much before the auditor. Cast includes husband, wife, and a tax preparer and auditor who could both be male or female. Runs eight minutes.

THE SEA BREEZE RETIREMENT HOME — 32

Two men and two women are seated in the dining room of the Retirement Center where they live. Laughter ensues as they become acquainted, order their meals, discuss other residents, and hear the Activity Director and CEO make announcements over the intercom regarding the rules and regulations at the Center. Cast includes two men, two women, and an Activity Director and CEO who speak off-stage and could be men or women. Runs eight minutes.

DOLLARS AND SENSE — 40

Two wealthy women visit a financial advisor, who seeks to learn how they each acquired their wealth, how they spend it, and how they wish to invest it. However, the women have different ideas than the advisor on prudent investments. Cast includes two women and an advisor who could be a man or woman. Runs eight minutes.

ADAM AND EVE...WHAT IF? — 48

Adam awakes with a sore rib and a puzzling new partner, Eve, who talks too much, questions his decisions, has ideas of her own about living in Paradise, and has a job list for Adam. This is the first of three skits and a monologue that can make up a complete show of Bible stories with a comical twist. Cast includes a man, a woman, and God, who speaks offstage. Runs nine minutes.

FORTY DAYS AND FORTY NIGHTS — 58

Noah and his wife discuss life on the Ark, the animals, and the job duties of their three sons and their wives. Skit ends when the rain stops and the rainbow appears. Cast includes a man and a woman. Runs nine minutes.

SAMSON AND DELILAH 68

Handsome, proud, and conceited Samson meets beautiful, seductive, and crafty Delilah as she plys him with flattery, tricks, and riddles to get him to reveal the secret of his strength. Cast includes a man and a woman. Runs eleven minutes.

JONAH AND THE WHALE 80

Jonah tells of a directive from God that he didn't want to obey so he headed in the other direction, only to end up in the belly of a whale, who treated him to a bumpy ride and a bad breath that a case of mints wouldn't solve. Cast of one. Runs two minutes.

THE EXTENDED WARRANTY CALL 82

A housewife receives one of those bothersome sales calls and uses the opportunity to share all her troubles with the caller, while the caller tries frantically to turn the conversation back to the extended warranty she wishes to sell. Cast of two. Runs two minutes.

THE OLD WOMAN IN THE SHOE 85

The old woman defends herself against the impression one gets from the familiar nursery rhyme. She shares her life in the shoe and why she has so many children. Cast of one. runs two minutes.

Royalty Payment Form

ROYALTIES are due every time a skit is performed, even more than once, for an audience, recitation or public reading, paying or non-paying, professional or amateur. Author Jean Mosby hereby gives permission to reproduce cast copies for any skit for which royalties are paid as shown below. Please complete this form and submit it with your check to: Jean Mosby, 900 Tamiami Trail S., Apt. 424, Venice, FL 34285-3626.

Name: _____
Organization: _____
_____
Address: _____
_____
Phone: _____
E mail: _____
Performance dates: _____
_____

A Weekend in the Country: $15 x # of performances _____   = $ _____
Marriage Enrichment Counselor: $15 x # of performances _____   = $ _____
The Income Tax Audit: $15 x # of performances _____   = $ _____
Sea Breeze Retirement Home: $15 x # of performances _____   = $ _____
Dollars and Sense: $15 x # of performances _____   = $ _____
Adam and Eve...What If?: $15 x # of performances _____   = $ _____
Forty Days and Forty Nights: $15 x # of performances _____   = $ _____
Samson and Delilah: $15 x # of performances _____   = $ _____
Jonah and the Whale: $5 x # of performances _____   = $ _____
Extended Warranty Call: $5 x # of performances _____   = $ _____
Old Woman in the Shoe: $5 x # of performances _____   = $ _____

Total Payment = $ _____

Questions or comments welcome at mosbyseniorskits@gmail.com. We'd love to hear from you.
Have fun doing your shows!

This book is dedicated to Dr. Pam Kiefert Weiss, the professional director who first brought Readers' Theater to my retirement village, who gave me my first role in a Readers' Theater show, who taught me what little I know about acting, who suggested I try my hand at writing comedy skits, and who suggested I publish my skits. I thank Pam for her encouragement and friendship as I learned to love and appreciate how Readers' Theater can enrich one's life.

A Weekend in the Country

by Jean Mosby

CAST:

DELMAR: A milquetoast personality, driver of the car, husband of Jennifer
JENNIFER: Quick to tell others, including her husband Delmar, what to do
BRUCE: Caustic, know-it-all husband of Susan, who recently moved with Susan next door to Delmar and Jennifer
SUSAN: Prim and proper lady, wife of Bruce
SIRI: The GPS voice who wears a beanie with two antennas

AT RISE: Delmar is driving the car with Jennifer, Bruce, and Susan as passengers. Siri sits a bit off to the side.

DELMAR: Well, we're two hours into our first trip together. Sorry about the late start, but we'll have a great weekend in the country.

BRUCE: We would have started on time if your wife hadn't brought so much luggage. It wouldn't all fit in the trunk.

SUSAN: I'm sure Bruce doesn't mind sitting on his suitcase.

BRUCE: Hrump! My bottom feels like a dented fender.

SIRI: Proceed on State Highway 103 for five miles.

SUSAN: Imagine! A whole weekend relaxing together at a lakeside resort. I'm surprised you were able to get a reservation on such short notice.

JENNIFER: The resort brochure looks wonderful. Delmar! Watch out for that truck!

DELMAR: I see it Jennifer.

JENNIFER: You just missed it by a hair.

DELMAR: If you say so, dear.

BRUCE: Missed it by a mile.

JENNIFER: It looks different from up front.

BRUCE: Delmar, you just missed the turn on to County Road 56.

DELMAR: No, I put the route into the GPS and we are taking Hwy. 32 to I-23.

BRUCE: My smartphone tells me that Highway 56 is a shorter way.

DELMAR: Well, if you say so, I'll turn around. *(Everyone leans to the left as he turns the steering wheel.)*

SIRI: Recalculating. Make a U-turn at the next available intersection.

JENNIFER: I have a triptik from AAA and they say to take Hwy. 32.

DELMAR: Well, I'll turn around. *(Everyone leans to the right as he turns the steering wheel.)*

SIRI: Recalculating. Take a left on Hwy. 32.

BRUCE: Hrmph!   I knew I should have driven.

SUSAN: Won't it be wonderful to get to know each other better. Ever since we moved in next door to you last winter, we have been wanting to get better acquainted.

BRUCE: Our dog Woofy just had six puppies that look just like your dog Spikey. That's enough getting acquainted.

JENNIFER: Your Woofy came into our back yard and seduced Spikey.

SUSAN: Let's just say, "What happens in your backyard stays in your backyard."

JENNIFER: Well, you can tell your Woofy to quit making deposits in our yard. We're not a bank. Delmar, why don't you pass that truck?

DELMAR: There is a solid yellow line.

JENNIFER: No one is looking. If you hurry, you'll get around.

DELMAR: OK, dear. *(Turns the wheel to pass and all lean to left)*

SIRI: Approaching right turn onto the I-23 ramp.

BRUCE: You are in the left lane. You are going to miss the turn. County road 56 would have been much safer.

JENNIFER: Delmar, speed up. Hang on everybody. *(Turns the steering wheel and everyone jerks forward)*

SUSAN: Bruce, get off my neck and back on your suitcase.

BRUCE: In a minute. There's a wheel imprinted on my thigh.

JENNIFER: Everyone makes a little mistake now and then. It should be a smooth ride now that we are on I-23.

BRUCE: I need a cigarette. *(Gets out his pack)*

JENNIFER: Sorry, not in the car.

BRUCE: I'll just crack the back window.

JENNIFER: No way. I just had my hair done.

BRUCE: Some weekend! *(Putting his pack away)* Delmar, do you see that billboard for the Risque Cafe? Look at the gorgeous girl saying "We bare all."

SUSAN: We bare all. I wonder what that means.

JENNIFER: Does it need an explanation?

SUSAN: Maybe it's a counseling service where you can bare your deepest secrets.

BRUCE: Maybe we should stop and see. It's at this exit.

SUSAN: Maybe the Risque Cafe is a coffee shop.

BRUCE: Turn off here. We need a coffee break.

SUSAN: Good idea. I need a ladies room.

DELMAR: OK. *(Turns the steering wheel and all lean to right)*

SIRI: Recalculate. Take a U-turn at the next available opportunity.

JENNIFER: Delmar, you get back on I-23 immediately.

DELMAR: Yes, dear. *(Turns the steering wheel and all lean to left)*

BRUCE: Party pooper! Look! There's a Bass Pro Shop. That reminds me of our honeymoon.

DELMAR: How can a Bass Pro Shop remind you of your honeymoon?

SUSAN: He promised me two weeks in a romantic setting. Just the two of us. It sounded like a dream come true to me.

BRUCE: Well, it would have been if the tent hadn't leaked.

SUSAN: After the first night of rain he pitched the tent on a hill.

BRUCE: During the night I reached out to her and she was gone.

SUSAN: I slid down the hill and out the front flap.

BRUCE: Well you did enjoy the campfire cooking. Remember that wonderful stew I made over the open campfire?

SUSAN: No, I just remember scrubbing the blackened pot.

JENNIFER: Sounds like loads of fun.

BRUCE: Well, we were on a tight budget.

SUSAN: Yes, he gave me his ex-wife's diamond ring.

DELMAR: Susan, how long have you two been married?

SUSAN: Just three years. This is my second marriage.

JENNIFER; He wouldn't have been my first choice either. *(Smirking)*

BRUCE: You owe me an apology.

JENNIFER: Well, you aren't gonna get one. Delmar! Brake! That passing car cut back in too close.

DELMAR: Yes, dear. *(All lurch forward)*

JENNIFER: Bruce, get your head off my neck and get back on your suitcase.

BRUCE: Gladly.

JENNIFER: My triptik says there is a speed trap the next ten miles. Better slow down.

DELMAR: OK. Uh, oh! There is a disabled vehicle up ahead. We should stop and help.

BRUCE: No, we could waste a lot of time. Drive on.

DELMAR: The driver is signaling to us for help. She's all alone and has a flat tire.

SUSAN: What a beautiful young woman.

JENNIFER: Her shorts are way too tight.

BRUCE: We need to be good Samaritans. Delmar, stop!

JENNIFER: Delmar, you drive right on. We are on a tight schedule.

BRUCE: Party pooper!

JENNIFER: Delmar, you are driving too close to the garbage truck ahead of us. Why don't you pass him?

DELMAR: As soon as that line of semi's gets past, dear.

SUSAN: It's getting cold back here. Would you mind turning down the air conditioner?

JENNIFER: I'm very comfortable. Can't you put on a sweater?

SUSAN: Delmar, if you stop I'll get it out of my suitcase.

DELMAR: I'll turn down the air conditioner.

BRUCE: I'm getting hungry. Isn't it time to stop for lunch?

SUSAN: Yes, I need a ladies room.

DELMAR: I guess we could. Where would you like to stop?

BRUCE: My smart phone tells me there is a Longhorn Steakhouse at Exit 79. My stomach is begging for a juicy steak.

JENNIFER: I don't eat meat. Let's find a natural foods cafe and have a vegetarian sandwich?

SUSAN: I can't eat bread. I'm gluten intolerant. Let's just stop for a bowl of soup?

DELMAR: How about a Chinese place? You can have hot and sour soup or egg drop soup?

BRUCE: No Chinese food for me. I'm allergic to MSG.

DELMAR: There's a billboard for a Jack Daniel's Distillery tasting tour at this exit. I'm taking the exit and we're having lunch at Jack Daniel's Distillery. *(Turns the steering wheel and all lean to right)*

SIRI: Recalculate. Make a U-turn as soon as possible.

JENNIFER: I have no intention of drinking my lunch, Delmar.

DELMAR: Yes, dear. *(Turns the steering wheel and all lean to left)* We're getting close to the resort you reserved. Let's wait to have lunch there.

SUSAN: *(Desperately)* I need a ladies room.

JENNIFER: Hold off a little longer. We're almost there.

BRUCE: It's cooking in here. Turn up the air.

DELMAR: OK.

SUSAN: Jennifer, tell us about the resort.

JENNIFER: The brochure says that Shady Grove Resort is a rustic, woodsy retreat on a small lake ten miles from Pickett Corners, the nearest town.

SUSAN: Oh, a sand bar would be a lovely place to relax and enjoy the lake.

BRUCE: That's not the kind of bar I'm looking for.

DELMAR: Maybe we can rent a canoe.

BRUCE: That's so boring. Let's rent a motorboat or jet skis!

SIRI: Right turn approaching on County Road F.

JENNIFER: The resort instructions say it's two more exits.

DELMAR: We'd better turn here. *(Turns the steering wheel and all turn to right)*

BRUCE: This is the middle of nowhere. I think you turned too soon.

SUSAN: Does that broken sign say "Pickett Corners one-half mile?" Surely they will have a ladies room.

DELMAR: I'll stop for gas at the Pickett Corners Gas and Grocery Store.

SUSAN: Great. They'll have a restroom.

BRUCE: It seems to be closed. So is everything else in this hick town.

JENNIFER: Be patient. We're almost at the Shady Grove Resort.

SIRI: Right turn in five hundred yards.

DELMAR: Here is our turn. *(Turns wheel and all lean to the right)*

BRUCE: This can't be right. It's a gravel road. I'll Google it just to be sure.

SUSAN: Good idea. There's a bush. Can we stop for a minute?

SUSAN: Hold on. We're almost there.

BRUCE: No phone service.

SIRI: Private road. No further directions.

SUSAN: I have to go.

BRUCE: Not out here you don't.

JENNIFER: Hold on just a little longer. Oh, there it is up ahead!

SUSAN: It looks **very** rustic. *(With disappointment)*

DELMAR: The front porch is sagging.

BRUCE: The whole place needs painting.

JENNIFER: Don't get out of the car. There is a strange dog coming toward us.

BRUCE: It's a pot-bellied pig!

SUSAN: The lake is full of bull rushes. And there is no beach.

JENNIFER: At least there is a row of little blue changing stations just past the back door.

BRUCE: Those are porta potties.

SUSAN: Well, I'm not going in there.

ALL: Turn around. Let's go home!

SIRI: Oh, no. Three more hours with these people. I have a migraine.

The Marriage Enrichment Counseling Session

by Jean Mosby

CAST:

MARGE, the Marriage Counselor
EDNA WHITMAN, the wife
SID WHITMAN, the husband

SCENE: Marge's Office

MARGE: Good morning, Mr. & Mrs. Whitman.

EDNA: Please call us Edna and Sid.

MARGE: And you may call me Marge. What brings you to the Marriage Enrichment Counseling Center?

EDNA: Well, Marge, the marriage has gone a little stale over the years and we thought we might, you know, liven it up a bit.

SID: Yeah, marriage can be fun some of the time. Trouble is, you're married all of the time.

EDNA: Sid!

MARGE: I like to think of marriage as a ring.

SID: Like a three-ring circus?

THE MARRIAGE ENRICHMENT COUNSELING SESSION

MARGE: Not exactly. First comes the engagement ring. Then comes the wedding ring...

SID: Then comes the suffer..ring.

MARGE: Well, that is certainly a new definition.

SID: Marriage is like a midnight phone call. You get a ring and then you wake up.

EDNA: Marge, he's just joking. Sid has been a good husband.

SID: Of course. Being a husband is like any other job. It helps if you like the boss.

MARGE: Sid, Edna would like to see some changes in your relationship. How do you feel about that? For example, more communication or more transparency?

SID: Transparency is the clear choice but...I don't want to talk about it.

MARGE: Sometimes talking can relieve...

SID: Every time I do something she doesn't like...I don't want to talk about it.

MARGE: It's OK if you don't want to talk about it. We can go on...

SID: Yesterday when I came home a little late...I don't want to talk about it.

MARGE: Men are often more reluctant to discuss their feelings, so don't be embarrassed...

SID: Right after we got married she...I don't want to talk about it.

MARGE: Let's go back to when your marriage began. Tell me about your feelings then.

SID: When Edna and I were first married, Edna would bring me a beer and our cute little dog would run around yipping and barking. Now, the dog brings me the beer and Edna yips and barks.

EDNA: What are you complaining about? You are getting the same service, aren't you?

SID: I'm not complaining, dear. Just stating the facts.

EDNA: Well, before Sid proposed I was asked to get married several times.

SID: Oh, yeah, who asked you to get married?

EDNA: My mom and dad.

SID: I was encouraged when her dad said, "Sid, I think Edna should get married." But then he said, "I don't think she should marry you."

EDNA: Well, Sid proposed anyway.

MARGE: Edna, tell me about how Sid proposed.

EDNA: Well, we were sitting on the couch. He was really nervous and just blurted out, "I think we should get married." I said, "That's not much of a proposal. I think you can do better than that."

SID: And I said, "I don't know. Your sister Sue already said no."

EDNA: Well, I certainly did better than Sue. Her first husband Joe had spent time in prison.

MARGE: Really, tell me about that.

EDNA: Well, Joe was married twice before.

MARGE: Did he get divorced from both his wives?

EDNA: No, they both died.

MARGE: Oh, I am sorry to hear that. What did the first wife die of?

EDNA: Mushrooms.

THE MARRIAGE ENRICHMENT COUNSELING SESSION

MARGE: Mushrooms? That sounds suspicious. Did the second wife die of mushrooms?

EDNA: No. She died of a fractured skull.

MARGE: Oh, good grief! What on earth happened to her?

EDNA: She wouldn't eat the mushrooms.

MARGE: I can understand why he went to prison. I would say Sue used pretty poor judgment in marrying him. Why did she marry him?

SID: They met at a travel agency. She was looking for a vacation and he was the last resort.

EDNA: Well, she couldn't know that at the time.

SID: We couldn't decide what to give them for their wedding.

EDNA: I said, "I give them two weeks." Actually the marriage lasted two months.

SID: Then she married Harry.

MARGE: How did that marriage turn out?

EDNA: Pretty good. After all these years he still calls her "Darling," "Honey," and "Love."

SID: That's because he forgot her name ten years ago and he's scared to ask.

EDNA: Harry is good to Sue. Two times a week they go out to a nice restaurant and have a little wine and good food.

SID: Sue goes on Tuesdays and Harry goes on Fridays.

MARGE: Well, I'm glad it worked out.

SID: That's why Edna considers me a pretty good catch.

MARGE: How long have you been married?

SID: We've been happily married for thirty years.

EDNA: Thirty years isn't bad, considering we just celebrated our fiftieth.

MARGE: Marriage does have its ups and downs but we learn a lot from a marriage of such long duration. Marriage teaches you loyalty, forbearance, meekness, self-restraint, and forgiveness.

EDNA: Qualities I wouldn't have needed if I had stayed single.

MARGE: Well, let's see if we can locate why the spark has left your marriage. Have you been experiencing any particular problems? Sid, do you wake up grumpy in the mornings?

SID: No, I generally let Edna sleep in.

EDNA: Well, there was one big one that we haven't resolved yet. You know, Sid, the Julia episode.

MARGE: I suppose you are talking about an infidelity issue.

SID: Not really. It was just a trivial thing. I just said to her, "Can you bring me a glass of water, Julia?"

EDNA: My name is not Julia.

MARGE: Who is Julia?

SID: Just an old girlfriend from high school.

EDNA: Well, you must still be dreaming about her.

THE MARRIAGE ENRICHMENT COUNSELING SESSION

SID: Sometimes Edna gets jealous of my old girlfriends. Last week we saw Bubbles Jones at a restaurant's bar. I told Edna she had nothing to worry about. Bubbles has been drinking like that since I left her years ago.

EDNA: That's impossible. Nobody celebrates that long!

SID: If you want to talk about unresolved issues, how about the time I had my knee replacement surgery and you kept talking behind my back?

EDNA: What did you expect? I was pushing you in a wheelchair.

MARGE: What did you two do for a living?

SID: I was an engineer and Edna was a housewife.

MARGE: Do you consider that you have an equal partnership when it comes to household duties since you retired?

EDNA: Usually I do the laundry. Tuesday, I pulled the laundry out of the washer and found a $50 dollar bill in Sid's pocket.

SID: Yah! I accused her of money laundering!

EDNA: But I put the clean $50 dollar bill in my purse.

SID: I do a lot of the household management. For instance, I am cooking in the microwave and doing the vacuuming, all while I am on the cell phone reading about conspiracy theories.

EDNA: Yes, those who conspire are watching us alright! But the real culprit is something else! That vacuum has been collecting personal dirt for years!

SID: Of course. I was watching Edna make breakfast one morning and I noticed that she made way too many trips to get each of the items she needed.

EDNA: Of course. He wants a big breakfast.

SID: So I said in my kindest Engineer's voice, "Hey, sweetheart, why don't you utilize the load maximization principle and carry all the items you need in one trip, thereby minimizing total distance traveled?"

EDNA: I loved his suggestion. It used to take me eleven minutes to make breakfast. Now he does it in five. Works for me.

MARGE: Who cleans up and loads the dishwasher?

EDNA: When Sid cooks, I clean up and do the dishes. But we don't have a dishwasher because I don't trust them to get the dishes clean, so I wash them by hand.

SID: When Edna cooks, I clean up and do the dishes. You say we don't have a dishwasher? Then what's that thing where I've been putting the dishes?

EDNA: Oh, that's why I found scrambled eggs and bits of bacon in the spa this afternoon.

MARGE: Edna, do you feel that Sid listens when you express a problem?

SID: I do listen and respond to Edna's requests. She texted me at the bowling alley one cold winter morning saying, "Windows frozen, won't open." I texted her back to gently pour some hot water along the edges and tap it with a hammer.

EDNA: Yes, and I texted back, "Computer is really messed up now."

MARGE: Do you offer each other compliments?

SID: Of course, I am very quick to compliment Edna. When she stood in front of the mirror and complained, "I look old, fat, and wrinkled. I really need you to pay me a compliment," I quickly replied, "Your eyesight is darn near perfect."

MARGE: There are many ways to show a woman that you love her. Some women prefer words. Others prefer a willing helper. Some respond best to receiving a gift. Do you give each other gifts?

THE MARRIAGE ENRICHMENT COUNSELING SESSION

SID: For our fortieth wedding anniversary I wanted to get her flowers but a bouquet of roses cost $80. So I went to the supermarket to get her flowers.

EDNA: Oh, whoopee! Two bags of Pillsbury unbleached for $4.99.

SID: Well, I gave her a hint of what I wanted for our fortieth anniversary.

EDNA: He said, "I want something shiny that goes from 0-100 in three seconds."

SID: She bought me a digital scale.

MARGE: Well, I see we have some work to do on communication.

SID: And when I took her to an orchard and we stood there staring at the rows and rows of fruit trees for more than an hour, she said, "This is not what I meant when I was expecting an Apple Watch for my birthday."

MARGE: I am sure she did not mean to be unappreciative of your efforts. It was just a misunderstanding. Shall we move on to activities that you share? What do you two do for fun together?

SID: I said, "Let's go out tonight and have some fun!"

EDNA: And I said, "Great idea! If you get back before I do, leave the lights on."

SID: Edna complains that my life revolves around football and she's sick of it. I don't understand. We've been together for fifty seasons and ten playoffs.

MARGE: Intimacy is very important in a marriage. How is your sex life?

SID: Hey, I am known down at the tavern as...

EDNA: Sure you are. When I say, "Honey, let's go upstairs and make love," he tells me, "Choose one. I can't do both."

SID: I'm pretty sensitive to my wife's needs. I told her to embrace her mistakes…and she hugged me!

MARGE: How about travel? Do you enjoy traveling together?

SID: We've traveled all over the world.

EDNA: Yes, to every country in Epcot.

MARGE: Do you have some local destinations that you both enjoy? Perhaps picnics at the lake or hikes in the forest? Maybe a favorite bar or restaurant?

EDNA: Sure, Sid and I went to the Ranch House down on Sixth Street. You know, the one noted for their steaks.

SID: When I order my steak and salad I always have a double order of mashed potatoes.

MARGE: Sounds like you enjoy mashed potatoes.

SID: No, Edna always orders just a steak and salad to keep her carbs low and then eats half of my mashed potatoes.

EDNA: I do not! I read that women who carry a little weight live longer than men who mention it.

SID: I lost my credit card at the restaurant but I didn't report it. The thief is spending less than my wife.

SID: Edna complained that I was spending too much time at the local tavern, so one night I took her along. I asked her, "What'll you have?" She said "Oh, I don't know. The same as you, I suppose."

MARGE: That sounds like a fun evening.

THE MARRIAGE ENRICHMENT COUNSELING SESSION

EDNA: So he ordered a Jack Daniel for each of us and drank his down in one gulp. I watched him and tried the same thing but coughed, choked, and burned my throat." I said, "Yuck, this tastes awful, worse than awful."

SID: Well, there you go. And she thought I was out enjoying myself every night.

MARGE: Do you ever have friends in for drinks or dinner? Friends can add a great deal to keep a marriage interesting.

SID: Remember when I came home from playing golf one day and said, "Honey, I invited a friend home for dinner."

EDNA: And I said, "The house is a mess, all the dishes are dirty, and I don't have groceries to cook a meal. Why did you invite a friend for dinner tonight?"

SID: The poor fool was thinking of getting married.

EDNA: We have my brother Amos over for dinner often. Amos isn't the brightest bulb but he's very loving.

SID: Once when we invited Amos over, he got unruly. He kicked, screamed, and cursed.

MARGE: Sounds like he has quite a temper.

SID: Yes, it's the last time we invited him over to play Tiddleywinks.

EDNA: I must admit that Amos seems just a little strange sometimes.

SID: Yeah, his cheese has slid off his crackers.

EDNA: And we have my sister Sue and her husband Harry in for dinner often.

SID: But they won't come around much since last March when they came for dinner.

EDNA: Yes, and I worked so hard to get ready. I vacuumed, dusted, ran to the grocery store, and tidied up the house. Their six-year-old granddaughter Lulu came early to help me.

SID: When everyone was seated at the table I asked Lulu to say the prayer. She was shy and didn't know what to say. So I told her just to say what Edna says.

EDNA: So she prayed, "Lord, why did I ask these people to dinner."

MARGE: Many marriages are enriched by children. Do you have children?

SID: Edna and I have decided we don't want children. We will be telling them this weekend.

EDNA: Yes, after lots of thought we have reached the difficult decision that we don't want children. So we placed an ad in the paper and if an interested party contacts us, we will drop them off on Sunday.

MARGE: This is highly unusual. How old are your children and what are their names?

EDNA: We have twins, one boy and one girl, who just turned forty-five. Telling you their names involves a long story.

MARGE: We have just enough time to hear your story, and then I will wrap up our session and make a follow-up appointment.

EDNA: A couple of weeks before my due date my brother Amos was visiting and suddenly I had shooting pains in my abdomen.

SID: Unfortunately I was out of town for work so my brother-in-law Amos drove Edna straight to the hospital. While she was being examined, Amos called to let me know what was happening and I promised to be on the next flight home.

MARGE: Just what a caring husband would do.

THE MARRIAGE ENRICHMENT COUNSELING SESSION

SID: When I arrived at the hospital Amos was waiting at the door to inform me that the twins were born but the birth was rough and Edna had passed out as soon as they were born.

EDNA: While I was out cold, the nurse came in with the birth certificate and asked for the twins' names, so Amos went ahead and chose them for us.

SID: I was relieved that everyone was OK but a little concerned that Amos had chosen my children's names. So I asked what names he had chosen. For the girl he chose Denise, which I actually liked.

MARGE: And what name did Amos choose for the boy?

SID: DeNephew.

MARGE: I can understand why this was upsetting. Thank you for sharing so much during our session today. We have a number of issues we can work on in future sessions.

EDNA: Oh, good, we can come back again.

MARGE: Yes, you have a lot of potential for improving your marriage and you both seem very willing to work on it. I'll set you up for next Tuesday at 10:00.

SID: Edna, this has been great reminiscing about our fifty years together. Let's come back again. In fact, it would be helpful if we bring all the family. We can bring Amos, and Sue and Harry.

EDNA: I'll bet Denise and DeNephew would enjoy telling about their lives.

MARGE: Oh, no! *(Reacts in horror)*

The Income Tax Audit

by Jean Mosby

CAST:

HOMER WALKER: Sly, arrogant, over-confident small business owner, dressed with loud clothing and baseball hat

DEBBIE WALKER: Homer's naive but excited wife who can't keep her mouth shut, overdressed in somewhat gaudy clothes with hat and scarf

ALICE: The Walker's income tax preparer dressed in business attire, who becomes increasingly frustrated with the talkative Walkers

DAN WHITE: IRS agent, dressed in business attire, all business. This character could be played by a woman, DENISE.

SCENE: Homer and Debbie are seated in an IRS office with an empty chair between them and an empty chair beside Debbie.

HOMER: Here we are at the Internal Revenue Service office for our first audit. The guys down at the bar will be waiting to hear all about it. Yah, my buddy Ralphie says, "There is a difference between a taxidermist and a tax collector. The taxidermist only takes the skin."

DEBBIE: Yep, the President's speech last night called for a complete overhaul of the tax code.

HOMER: He was shocked to find some millionaires in this country were still paying taxes.

DEBBIE: Isn't it exciting to be at our first IRS audit. I can't wait to tell the bridge group all about it. Myrtle told us that 65% of people say that cheating on your income tax is worse than cheating on your spouse.

THE INCOME TAX AUDIT

HOMER: I'll bet the other 35% were wives.

DEBBIE: The only difference between death and taxes is that Congress doesn't meet every year to make death worse.

ALICE: *(Enters and is seated between Homer and Debbie)* What are you two doing here? I asked you not to come to the audit. As your tax preparer, I prefer to handle it myself.

DEBBIE: Oh, please, Alice. We just couldn't stay away. It's so exciting.

HOMER: Where is the auditor anyway? This should be a piece of cake and I can't wait to get it started.

ALICE: *(Hesitating)* OK. IRS Agent Dan should be with us shortly. Let's take this time to review some important things we talked about earlier.

DEBBIE: Absolutely.

ALICE: When I prepared your tax return last April, I questioned some of the figures you gave me. But you assured me you have adequate records to support them. Have you sent those records that Agent Dan requested?

HOMER: You bet. There won't be any problem.

ALICE: And when you brought me the letter from IRS saying that your return is being audited, I stressed the importance of letting me go into the audit for you alone.

DEBBIE: We remember.

ALICE: I have been preparing income tax returns for thirty years. I have handled many audits for my clients and have worked with Agent Dan White many times.

HOMER: I remember that you preferred to handle the audit alone and asked us not to come along. But we wouldn't miss it.

ALICE: Since you insist on being here, I must warn you to let me answer the questions. Do **not** offer any additional information.

DEBBIE: Oh, we'll be so good. You can count on us.

ALICE: Then we are agreed that I will handle the audit and you will simply observe. If I feel you are interfering or causing us to go off track, I will give you a signal.

DEBBIE: Oh, we promise, don't we Homer?

HOMER: Scout's honor.

ALICE: Good. Now, I must ask you once again about underreporting income on your business. It appears clear to me from the amount of product that you buy that you are not reporting all your sales. This will be very evident to the auditor as well.

HOMER: *(Winking)* Underreporting of income? Maybe a little fudging here and there. That's all.

DEBBIE: George Washington never told a lie, but then he never had to fill out a Form 1040.

HOMER: Even if we were cheating, you know how clueless these IRS guys are.

DEBBIE: Homer, tell Alice what Ralphie said about the IRS agent on the cruise.

HOMER: Well, one evening an IRS agent was walking by a travel agent's office and saw a poster in the window that said, "World Cruise, $200."

DEBBIE: *(Excitedly)* So he went in, signed up, and paid his $200.

HOMER: Suddenly a big brute of a man sneaked up behind him and hit him on the head with a mallet, knocking him out.

DEBBIE: Out like a light!

THE INCOME TAX AUDIT

HOMER: The unconscious agent was loaded into a truck, hauled to the beach, and, still unconscious, set adrift on a raft. The next morning he woke up, looked across the sea, and saw another man in a raft drifting off in the distance.

DEBBIE: And the agent yelled, "Are you on the World Cruise?" And the other guy yelled back, "Yes I am."

DEBBIE: And the agent called out, "Do you know what time they serve breakfast?"

HOMER and DEBBIE: *(Laughing heartily)*

ALICE: Please don't tell Agent Dan any jokes.

DAN: *(Enters and sits beside Debbie)* Good morning Mr. and Mrs. Walker. I am Dan White and I will be doing the audit on your last year's tax return.

HOMER: *(Still laughing)* Howdy, Dan.

ALICE: Good morning, Dan.

DAN: Let's begin by verifying some routine details. You are Homer and Debbie Walker, a married couple living at 215 Oakbrook Circle in Lake City, MN.

ALICE: That is correct Agent Dan, they have been--

DEBBIE: Well, actually we are no longer married. We have been divorced for three years.

ALICE: *(Tapping her lips as she looks at Debbie)* This is news to me.

DAN: But you have been filing your tax returns as Married Filing Joint.

HOMER: Heh, heh. Boy did we save a lot of money over filing as single people.

ALICE: *(Tapping lips at Homer)* Homer, please.

DAN: Let me get your correct addresses then. Who lives at 215 Oakbrook Circle?

DEBBIE: We both do. I live on the first floor with my boyfriend Fred and Homer lives on the second floor with his girlfriend Judy.

ALICE: *(Sighing with frustration)* I am feeling faint.

DAN: How does that work?

DEBBIE: I cook on Monday, Wednesday, and Friday. Judy cooks on Tuesday, Thursday, and Saturday. We go out together Sundays.

DAN: Not Married Filing Jointly. *(Dryly)* Duly noted.

HOMER: *(Sarcastically)* Duly noted.

DAN: What is your occupation?

ALICE: Homer is a bus driver at the local high school and Debbie is an assistant at the Happy Times Day Care Center. During the summer they operate a small hamburger stand at the lake.

DEBBIE: Agent Dan, you should drop by some time and taste our burgers. People flock to our stand all summer long just to experience my grandma Helen's special recipe. Tender, juicy burgers topped with a special sauce.

ALICE: *(Makes a move to control Debbie)* Just hamburgers and sodas, that's what they sell.

DAN: Let's have a look at your Schedule C where you report your income and expenses. I see you are claiming a large loss last year. What is your markup?

HOMER: Markup? A burger costs us $5 to make and we sell it for $10.

DAN: I see. Then if you bought $30,000 worth of hamburger your sales should be $60,000.

THE INCOME TAX AUDIT

DEBBIE: Makes sense to me.

DAN: But you didn't report sales of $60,000. You reported $10,000 less.

ALICE: Uh, oh! Here we go. Dan, I believe I can shed some light on that situation. The Walkers are inexperienced cooks and managers--

HOMER: I can explain. We eat a lot of it ourselves. And we have my relatives in for burgers on holidays.

ALICE: *(Makes a move to control Homer)* Dan, what they mean to say is...

DEBBIE: And my brother Al and his wife Sarah and their eight kids come by on the Fourth of July and Labor Day. They bring the salad and dessert and we supply the free burgers.

ALICE: *(Silently mouthes)* Shut up!

DAN: Eight kids, you say?

HOMER: Yeah, Sarah watches too much of that sexy TV show Desperate Housewives.

DEBBIE: It's not that so much as Al. He can get frisky watching HGTV.

HOMER: Al is pretty proud of his brood of kids.

DEBBIE: Well, you know, a rooster crows but a hen delivers.

ALICE: *(Becoming increasingly frustrated)* Can we please move on with the audit?

HOMER: Don't ever take a driving trip with them. They stop a lot.

DEBBIE: Yeah, their license plate reads PB4WEGO.

HOMER: Get it? PB4WEGO. Pee before we go. Heh, heh!

ALICE: *(Even more frustrated)* Please, let's get back to the audit.

DAN: Free giveaways to relatives. Underreported income. Duly noted.

HOMER: Duly noted.

DAN: Talking about children, let's move on to your dependents. You are claiming someone named Fluffy Walker.

DEBBIE: Homer, I told you not to claim the cat.

ALICE: *(Becoming frantic)* But you told me it was your niece who lives with you.

DAN: Cat, hmmm? Duly noted.

HOMER: Duly noted.

DAN: Now then, you also claim an elderly parent named Marvin Walker.

HOMER: That is my dad. Nicest old man you ever met.

DAN: And is he too old and feeble to live independently on his own?

DEBBIE: No, he's too dead.

ALICE: *(Moans)* Oh, no.

DAN: Just for the record, when did Marvin die?

HOMER: Three years ago.

ALICE: When this audit is over, I am going to retire.

HOMER: It was in August. He was in the hospital on his deathbed.

DEBBIE: We called his preacher to be with him in his final moments. As the preacher stood steadfastly by the bed, Marvin's condition seemed to deteriorate, and Marvin motioned frantically for someone to pass him a pen and paper.

HOMER: The preacher quickly got a pen and paper and handed it to Marvin. But before the preacher had a chance to read the note, Marvin died.

DEBBIE: Yep, poor old dad, just up and died. The Preacher felt that it wasn't the right time to read it so he put the note in his jacket pocket.

HOMER: It was at the funeral, while speaking, that the Preacher suddenly remembered the note.

DEBBIE: He reached deep into his pocket and said "And you know what, I suddenly remembered that right before Marvin died he handed me a note. Knowing Marvin I'm sure it was something inspiring from which we can all gain."

HOMER: With that introduction the preacher ripped out the note and opened it. The note said "Hey, you are standing on my oxygen tube."

DAN: Two less dependents. Duly noted.

HOMER: Duly noted.

DEBBIE: You asked about our children. Sherry, our only daughter is in California. What a brood of six grandkids. We keep in touch with them by smartphone every weekend.

HOMER: You ought to see the pictures they send. We are on the phones for hours.

DEBBIE: We fly out to see Sherry and her family each Christmas. What a time we have!

ALICE: *(Making another move to quiet Debbie)* But you told me--

DAN: That would explain the deduction for eight smartphones and the monthly charges for the phone packages buried here in your Entertainment Expenses. Duly noted.

HOMER: Duly noted.

DAN: Moving on to Travel Expenses, how would you explain the $2,000 airfare trip to California last December as a business expense?

HOMER: Oh, that's easy to explain. During the two week stay we checked out thirty-five McDonald's.

ALICE: *(Sobbing)* Thirty-five McDonalds?

DEBBIE: Got to keep up with the competition. We kept notes of each visit on our Smart phone calendar.

DAN: I did request you bring a printout of the daily log of your business visits in California. I'd like to examine that next.

DEBBIE: Sorry. Accidentally deleted. Computer malfunction.

ALICE: *(Screams)* Ahhhhhh!

DAN: No travel expenses allowed. Duly noted.

HOMER: Duly noted.

DAN: I believe that wraps it up. I'll be recalculating your returns as single taxpayers.

HOMER: *(Moaning)* Oh, no.

DAN: I'll raise income by $10,000, decrease Entertainment Expense by $8,000, reduce Travel Expense by $2,000, remove two dependents.

HOMER: Oh, no. Debbie, don't mention this to your bridge club.

DAN: That will increase your taxable Social Security. And we'll add penalty and interest.

DEBBIE: He's just like a cannibal tax auditor. Charges an arm and a leg.

DAN: I'll tally it all up and send a bill.

HOMER: Just like Ralphie said, "Tax shelters are like parking spots. As soon as you find one, it's gone." Let's go home Debbie.

ALICE: Homer, if you have any questions when you get the bill, don't call me. Call H&R Block.

DAN: Good. We finished in time for me to sign up for that World Cruise.

THE SEA BREEZE RETIREMENT HOME

by Jean Mosby

CAST:

HENRY: A new male resident who is quite the hypochondriac

SANDY: An attractive divorcee obsessed with diet, exercise and appearance and is looking for a new man in her life. Any man will do.

GERTIE: A sweet little lady with poor hearing who often misinterprets words.

ANNA: A female with failing memory and a tendency toward gossip

MS. MELODY: The company Resident Services Director who makes frequent announcements over the dining room sound system. Can be read offstage. A few melodious notes sound prior to each of her announcements.

MR. ALBERT: The company Manager who makes announcements over the dining room sound system, always first announced by Ms. Melody.

SCENE: Four residents are seated in the dining room at The Sea Breeze Retirement Home located on the shores of Florida's Gulf Coast.

SANDY: Hi, Anna. Hi, Gertie. Sir, this is the first time I've seen you here in the dining room at the Sea Breeze Retirement Home. Are you a new resident?

HENRY: Yes, I just moved from New York to the second floor of the new residential building named after our mayor, Ned Tide.

GERTIE: Indeed, the Red Tide has been really bad this year. But still, it's wonderful living on the shores of Florida's Gulf Coast.

ANNA: Hi, Henry. It's ninety-five degrees outside with eighty percent humidity and storm clouds threatening from the West, but welcome to sunny Florida, our tropical paradise.

SANDY: How nice to meet you, Henry. I am Sandy and I live right across the road from the Ned Tide building in the Stone Crab House, Apartment 134. And this is Gertie, who has lived here for twenty years in the Flipper Tail building.

GERTIE: Eh, what? Oh, yes, the mail has been late coming recently.

HENRY: Hello, everyone. And where do you live, Anna?

ANNA: I live across from your building in Fish Hook Hall.

GERTIE: You are quite tall for a man your age.

SANDY: Not only tall, but quite handsome.

MS. MELODY: *(Ding, dong)* Good afternoon Sea Breeze residents. This is Ms. Melody, your Resident Services Director. Our new manager, Mr. Albert, has cut our paper budget so instead of printing your menus, I will be announcing your meal choices. For your dining pleasure this evening we offer three entrees: liver and onions, lasagne, or salmon. Our starch offering is fries, mashed potatoes, a baked sweet potato or garlic bread. Your yummy veggie choices are spinach, turnip greens, or kale. Enjoy!

ANNA: Ah, here is our waitress, Flo. Flo, I will have a large cranberry juice, a small 2% milk, the soup of the day...no, wait a minute...change that to a small apple juice and a large milk...and I'll have the liver and onions and a small order of fries. No, wait...make that a half portion of liver but a whole portion of onions.

GERTIE: I'll just have whatever it was that Anna ordered, Flo.

HENRY: Flo, I will have the lasagne with the house salad and garlic bread.

ANNA: Flo, would you change that to the mashed potatoes instead of the fries...and I guess I'll skip the soup...and please bring me a glass of ice.

SANDY: Let's see how many points I have on my Weight Watcher's app. Liver is eight points...lasagne is nine points. Too much cheese. Hold on a minute, Flo. Salmon is free. OK, I'll have the salmon. Now let's see...sweet potato is four points, but spinach is zero. I'll have the spinach. Please have the chef steam it rather than grill it. We are what we eat, you know. Diet and exercise work together to keep a trim figure.

ANNA: Flo, did I say apple juice? Would you change it to prune juice? And please add an order of kale.

GERTIE: Why has Flo just thrown her order pad into the air? Now she is stomping on it!

MS. MELODY: *(Ding, dong)* Good evening residents. Our new Manager, Mr. Albert, would like a word.

MR. ALBERT: Hello, dear Sea Breeze residents. Important bulletins will no longer be placed in your cubbies, as they have been removed. We needed the space to hang the Board of Directors. Ah, ah, uh, pictures. I mean to say, "the Board of Directors' pictures." So I will be bringing my bulletins to you during dinner. On another note, due to our recent cost cutting action, I want to make this important announcement about a change in Transportation. In order to save gas and vehicle expenses, all trips to the Tampa airport will be made in the two-person golf cart. Additional passengers and luggage will be strapped on the roof. The $125 charge will continue to apply.

GERTIE: I see Bert and Fanny are splitting another meal. What a charming couple they are. They say they split everything fifty/fifty. Now he is putting half his meal on her plate.

HENRY: Look at him carefully cutting the hamburger in half. And now he is counting out the fries and dividing them one by one.

SANDY: Now Bert has poured half of his coffee into her cup. Now he is beginning to eat his half of the meal.

HENRY: But why is Fanny just sitting and watching, with her hands folded in her lap?

ANNA: Because it's his day to share the teeth.

MS. MELODY: *(Ding, dong)* An important bulletin just came in from Ms. Louise, your Food and Dining Director to our six hundred residents. As you know, our beautiful dining room seats just one hundred residents. To alleviate overcrowding we have extended the lunch hours from 9:30 a.m. till 3:00 p.m. Your dinner hours are extended from 3:30 p.m. till 8:00 p.m. Residents are encouraged to dine quickly as the tables will be turned every half hour.

ANNA: Ah, here is Flo with our dinner. No, dear I ordered the fries, not the mashed potatoes. No, it was the cranberry juice and a large milk. And why did you bring me just a half portion? *(Aside to Henry)* Oh, dear, I don't see why she never gets my order right!

HENRY: I can't imagine why.

ANNA: My liver and onions look delicious.

GERTIE: Eh, what? Are you having liver problems?

HENRY: I just got out of the hospital last month after having a bad liver attack. What a miserable time of vomiting, pain, and diarrhea. And after six days of that, the constipation set in.

ANNA: Ugh! I believe I am through with my liver and onions.

HENRY: *(Pulls out a pill pack)* I still have to take these little yellow liver pills each day. And my blood pressure was hitting 160/98 when I got home so now I take this pink pill. The blue one is for cholesterol. Two years ago I had a triple bypass.

GERTIE: The bypass on Highway 41 isn't finished yet.

MS. MELODY: *(Ding, dong)* Dear residents, Ms. Louise, your Food and Dining Coordinator, reminds you that there is a limit on food carry outs. The Food Police will be at the door as you exit. Your walkers will be inspected for contraband. Another bulletin just in, a reminder that Pokeno begins in twenty minutes. In lieu of cash prizes we will be offering some exciting new prizes: a large bottle of Geritol and a package of Depends.

GERTIE: Indeed, I depend on Geritol to give me the energy I need to carry on at my age.

SANDY: Did you hear that we have a new 8:00 p.m. curfew? Security will be locking us in promptly at 8:00.

ANNA: Yes, but there is a one-hour extension for Bingo night. By the way, did you hear about the new Bingo prizes? Boxes of Polident and thirty-two ounce bottles of prune juice.

HENRY: I guess I better start playing Bingo.

SANDY: Henry, do you enjoy the company of an intelligent and beautiful woman? There is one who stands out here, as you can see.

HENRY: See? I haven't been able to see well for five years since I had a little accident.

ANNA: Oh, dear. Tell us about it.

HENRY: It was a Friday afternoon when I left work, my paycheck in hand. Instead of going home to my dear wife Eleanor, now departed, bless her soul, I stayed out the entire weekend partying with the boys and spent my entire paycheck.

SANDY: Naughty you!

HENRY: When I finally arrived home Sunday night, I was confronted by Eleanor. She was very angry and barraged me for nearly two hours with a vicious tirade. Finally, she stopped nagging and simply said to me, "How would you like it if you didn't see me for two or three days?" I replied, "That would be fine with me." Monday went by and I didn't see my wife. Tuesday and Wednesday came and went and I didn't see her.

ANNA: Oh, my. Did she leave you?

HENRY: No, by Thursday the swelling went down just enough where I could see her a little out of the corner of my left eye.

SANDY: Well, I'm sorry to hear about your bad eyes, although I sense that you are a very passionate man, Henry.

HENRY: Not really, since I had my prostate problem. You can't imagine how painful it was. And now that I moved here I can't afford the Viagra. I feel like a newborn baby. No hair, no teeth, and I think I just wet my pants.

SANDY: Sounds like my ex-husband Oscar. We scheduled our annual medical exams on the same day. After Oscar's exam, he confided in the doctor. "After I have sex with my wife for the first time I'm usually hot and sweaty and then, after I have sex with my wife the second time, I am usually cold and chilly." When I followed with my exam, the doctor asked, "Your husband had an unusual concern. He claims that he is usually hot and sweaty after having sex the first time with you and then cold and chilly after the second time. Do you know why?" I replied, "Oh, that old coot! That's because the first time is usually in July and the second time is usually in December."

ANNA: Well, I'm content to stay single. Most of the men here are just looking for a nurse and a purse!

GERTIE: Did you say you lost your purse?

SANDY: Just look over there. Three tables to the right. Did you hear that those two are getting married? Imagine, at ninety-eight he is marrying a woman who is eighty-three. Must be a trophy wife. I hear Chaplain Dave is conducting the afternoon wedding out by the pond, with a reception to follow.

ANNA: They must be serving oatmeal and prunes at the reception.

GERTIE: Did you see the loons that took over the pond last week? They flew down from Minnesota for Spring Break.

SANDY: Did you hear that Mr. Albert has ordered the ambulances to turn off their sirens when they enter our campus. They were disrupting our naps.

MS. MELODY: *(Ding, dong)* This is an important announcement. It's hurricane season again here in Florida. Your Manager, Mr. Albert, reminds you of our hurricane plans. Should sheltering become necessary, you will move to the hallways. For your comfort while sheltering, Housekeeping will set up cots in the hallways. Males will sleep on even numbered floors and females will sleep on odd numbered floors. Hanky panky is strictly forbidden. Now, if the hurricane category exceeds a level three, we will be required to evacuate. Should the hurricane be moving up our Western Florida coast, buses will leave for the Happy Time Campground in Central Florida. Unless the hurricane moves up Central Florida, in which case buses will head for Miami. Unless the hurricane moves up the East Florida coast, we'll head for the Panhandle. Mr. Albert reminds us to be sure to pack our toothbrushes.

GERTIE: Bulrushes! Where are they sending us? To Egypt?

SANDY: Henry, it is quite romantic at the Happy Times Campground. A stroll around the moonlit lake with the right person can be lovely.

ANNA: Remember the last time we went there? Harry Headstrong went missing. Nurse Imogene ran everywhere looking for him. At first we thought the mosquitoes carried him off. Then she learned that he was last seen down by the lake. He was warned about that alligator in the lake.

GERTIE: It is getting late, but I can stay a bit longer.

MS. MELODY: *(Ding, dong)* Good evening once again, happy diners. Ms. Louise, your Food and Dining Room Director, reminds you of the new dress code. Your resident handbook states that shorts worn for our casual lunchtime dining must be approaching the knee. Your dining room host, Mr. McKnee, will be measuring. Thanks for volunteering, men, but we have it covered.

ANNA: Sandy, what have you been reading in your Book Club?

SANDY: Pretty boring stuff. Queen Victoria's biography. Sonya Sotomayer's autobiography. Michell Obama's *Becoming*. I was outvoted on *Fifty Shades of Gray* and *Lady Chatterley's Lover*. I dropped out and am taking the line dancing classes instead. At our last class we had twenty in our line.

GERTIE: Wine! I do love a good chardonnay. Flo, would you bring me a banana before I leave. Make it a yellow one. Don't bring me one with too many brown speckles. I really prefer a green one, but Ms. Louise considers it wasteful to give them to those over ninety-eight.

SANDY: It was nice to meet you, Henry. Would you like to drive out to the beach for an after-dinner drink? We could watch the sunset together.

HENRY: My cataracts are so bad I can't even see my coffee. My hands are so crippled I couldn't even mark an 'X' at election time. I can't turn my head because of the arthritis in my neck. My blood pressure pills make me so dizzy I can hardly walk.

SANDY: Well, count your blessings! You can still drive! Let's go.

MS. MELODY: *(Ding, dong)* And one last reminder, dear residents, from our Sea Breeze store managers. Our inventory now includes a generous supply of Tampax.

Dollars and Sense

by Jean Mosby

CAST:

DELLA, Financial Counselor
CORA, Wealthy divorcee
HELENE, Wealthy beneficiary

DELLA: Good morning. Welcome to the Dollars and Sense Financial Counseling Service. How can I help you ladies this morning?

CORA: I am Cora and this is Helene. We are thinking we need a little help with our finances. It is said that money talks, but all mine ever says is "Goodby."

HELENE: Yes, my money is getting tired. It doesn't want to work for me any more. I need help.

DELLA: Let's first talk about how you earn money. Then we can talk about how you spend your money. And then we can talk about how you invest your money.

CORA: That sounds like a good plan.

DELLA: Then let's begin with how you earn your money.

HELENE: I made my money the old fashioned way. I was very nice to my Great Aunt Sophie right before she died.

DELLA: I am sorry for your loss. How did your Aunt Sophie die?

HELENE: She died very unexpectedly. The police suspected foul play but no one was ever charged.

DELLA: Oh, dear. How much did you inherit?

HELENE: About two million in stock and the mansion, which is worth a million.

DELLA: And how about you Cora? How did you earn your money?

CORA: I divorced Sam, my husband of thirty years, and the bum gave me the house, the BMW, and a generous alimony for the rest of my life.

HELENE: And she deserves every cent. Sam got chummy with his secretary and started coming home late from work every night.

DELLA: I am so sorry. How did you discover the truth about his affair?

CORA: My first clue was the credit card receipt I found in his suit pocket for a diamond bracelet dated a week before our anniversary.

DELLA: Well, that was a generous anniversary gift.

CORA: He gave me a new vacuum cleaner for our anniversary.

DELLA: That must have been very painful for you.

CORA: Yes, it wasn't even a Hoover.

DELLA: Well, now that we have established the source of your income, let's move on to how you spend your money.

HELENE: Great! I certainly would like to find financial peace.

DELLA: Financial peace isn't the acquisition of things. It's learning to live on less than you make.

HELENE: I love money and I love spending it. I went right out after I got my inheritance and made some pretty good purchases. I invested in a diamond mine in Nigeria.

DELLA: How did you hear about the diamond mine?

HELENE: A man called me on the phone. Wasn't I lucky to have him pick me out of all the women in the world!

DELLA: So you never met the man?

HELENE: No, but I didn't need to. He had the nicest voice. Smooth, just like honey.

DELLA: I'll bet he did. Have you had a good return on the diamond mine?

HELENE: Not yet, the phone number has been disconnected.

DELLA: Hmmm. How else have you spent your inheritance?

HELENE: I bought my precious little dog Fifi a beautiful new dog house with electric lights, running water, and a fur-lined bed.

DELLA: Quite extravagant of you. Did Fifi like her new dog house?

HELENE: Unfortunately, the water pipes leaked and set off an electrical charge. May she rest in peace.

DELLA: My condolences on your loss.

HELENE: I purchased a new home in a better neighborhood.

CORA: Helene's neighbors haven't been welcoming. In fact, they are snobbish. I threw an open house reception for Helene and nobody came.

HELENE: We ate up leftover spinach dip and hot chicken wings for a week.

DELLA: Too many people spend money they earned to buy things they don't need to impress people they don't like.

HELENE: Yes, I found that money can't buy friends, but I did acquire a better class of enemies.

DELLA: Now, Cora, tell me how you spend your money.

CORA: I tried investing but it didn't work out. When I invested in a bull market I got gored. When I tried investing in a bear market I got mauled.

DELLA: That is a sad story. Yes, but the market can be very fruitful with the proper expertise to guide you. How else do you spend your money?

CORA: I don't drive so I hired a chauffeur for the BMW I got in the divorce.

HELENE: What a good looker she hired. Muscular, young, great sense of humor. He certainly knew his way around town.

CORA: He knew his way to Mexico with the BMW and the maid. I'm taking driving lessons.

DELLA: Let's move on to ways you can preserve your wealth. I'd like to help you build a portfolio that will give you a dividend income with capital gains over the years involving minimum risk.

CORA: Oh, I tried that and the year I invested in the stock market, it got an Olympic medal for diving.

HELENE: I hear that people are making a small fortune in Bitcoin.

DELLA: Most of the people who are making a small fortune in Bitcoin invested a large fortune in Bitcoin.

HELENE: But I want to make money fast.

DELLA: Investing should be more like grass growing or paint drying.

HELEN: Grass growing or paint drying. That's boring.

DELLA: If you want excitement, take your money to Las Vegas.

CORA: Been there, done that. Lost a lot but it sure was exciting.

DELLA: Let's start building a solid portfolio. I would suggest something in pharmacueticals. We'll start with Pfizer, who has a solid P/E ratio.

HELENE: A PU ratio?

DELLA: No, a P/E ratio. That is the ratio of Price to Earnings.

CORA: I wouldn't want to own Pfizer. They are making lots of money on the COVID shots and I object to getting COVID shots.

DELLA: All right then. How about General Mills. They have raised their dividend rate every year for the past twenty years. That would give you a steady income with great potential for capital growth.

HELENE: They make Cheerios. My ex-husband Sam ate Cheerios for breakfast every year of our thirty-year marriage. I couldn't possibly invest in General Mills.

CORA: How about Kellogg's cereal. I like their corn flakes with red berries.

DELLA: Kellog stock is listed as a Hold, not a Buy. We'll move on to another area. Let's look at Tyson Chicken. They have an excellent P/E ratio.

HELENE: I couldn't possibly own Tyson Chicken. Hundreds of the workers in their plants got COVID because Tyson didn't provide them with proper protection. No way will I be socially irresponsible and buy Tyson Chicken.

DELLA: Kimberly Clark is a good buy now. Consumer products are good staples to have in your portfolio.

CORA: What do they make?

DELLA: Diapers, toilet paper, paper towels, and other paper products that every household uses.

CORA: Believe me, I don't use diapers in my household. And think of all the trees that are cut down every year to keep this company in business.

HELENE: No, we couldn't have Kimberly Clark in our portfolio. What else do you suggest?

DELLA: Perhaps we could have a look at Amazon. They just did a 20 to 1 stock split to boost money into the company.

HELENE: If their stock split, it must have been damaged in the first place.

CORA: Amazon employees are not unionized. No way would I invest in a company that fights allowing their employees to unionize.

HELENE: How about Revlon stock? I love their new nail polish colors.

DELLA: The business news reported this morning that they are preparing to file for bankruptcy.

CORA: Oh, but their new lipstick colors are luscious. Surely their stock prices will go up again.

DELLA: Shall we look at the insurance industry? There is Allstate, State Farm, or Prudential. Would any of those interest you? Their end-of-quarter earnings are all positive.

HELENE: Well, I'm not investing in that company that runs the stupid ads with the emus.

CORA: Or the one with the guy who stumbles over the ads in front of the Statue of Liberty. Libbity bibbity.

DELLA: Do you have any particular companies that you favor?

CORA: We both like Coca Cola and would consider buying it.

DELLA: Coca Cola stock is listed as "Hold" right now but Pepsi is listed as a "Buy."

HELENE: No, absolutely, we like Coke products and wouldn't be caught dead owning Pepsi stock.

DELLA: Perhaps you would prefer to look at fixed investments rather than equities. Maybe something in municipals? There is a nice tax advantage to muni bonds. For instance, New York is offering some sanitary sewer improvement bonds to yield 4% but in your tax bracket that is equal to 6.2%.

HELENE: Sewer bonds. Yuck! What would my friends think if they knew I owned sewer bonds!

DELLA: Or New Orleans is offering water improvement bonds at a 4.2% yield. They would be a nice addition to your portfolio.

CORA: Sorry but I don't trust Southerners. I won't invest in any city south of the Mason Dixon line.

DELLA: Perhaps you would be interested in corporate bonds. CNN has a new CEO who is proposing a major expansion. Their recent bond issue yields 5.3% but in your tax bracket that would be an effective rate of 7.6%.

HELENE: CNN! You might as well ask me to invest in MSNBC! I don't trust the media and would never feel that my money was safe with them.

DELLA: In that case I might recommend at least a portion of your portfolio contain some U.S. Treasuries. They would be tax exempt on your state return.

HELENE: Good Heavens! I wouldn't trust the Government to pay me back.

CORA: Della, can we make another appointment to finish this discussion.

DELLA: Certainly. I'm sure we can find some investment suitable for each of you.

CORA: Great! Come on Helene. I have an appointment at the Cadillac dealer to shop for a new car. You can help me choose the color.

Adam and Eve. What if.....?

by Jean Mosby

CAST:

ADAM, in flesh-colored shirt
EVE, in flesh-colored shirt with leaves over breasts
GOD (Voice only)

SCENE: In the Garden of Eden

GOD: Adam, Adam, Adam *(Progressively louder)* Up and at'em. *(To self)* Oh, that's good. I'm going to keep that one.

ADAM: Oh, oh, yes! Hi, Your Honor, Most High, Master of the Universe, Sir, Boss Man, Head Honcho, El Jefe, The Big Bopper. What do I call you?

GOD: *(Somewhat impatiently)*: God! God will be fine.

ADAM: God. OK. Do you have a last name?

GOD: I do not. And it certainly isn't Damn.

ADAM: Yes, yes, of course God. What can I do for you?

GOD: It is what I can do for you, Adam. I want to give you a helpmate. Someone to keep you company, someone beautiful, someone to talk to, someone loving, someone to never start an argument, never pout, no tears...

ADAM: Oh, Oh, Oh, that sounds wonderful! Wow! But wait a minute, what's that going to cost me?

GOD: Over time, an arm and a leg!

ADAM: Whoa, whoa, whoa...what can I get for a rib???

GOD: Just go back to sleep and we will talk later. *(Adam falls asleep.)*

EVE: *(Waking up)* Oh, this is so nice! Beautiful, sunny day, smells so good, great day to be alive! I am going to explore! Where will I go? What will I do? What will I wear? I don't have a thing to wear! *(Looks down at her body)* I don't have anything on. I literally have nothing to wear! *(She sees Adam sleeping.)* Oh, my what is this?

ADAM: *(Arising sleepily, yawning)* What a good nap. Oh, I might have slept wrong. I am going to have to get one of those "My Pillows".

GOD: Adam, this is Eve. I gave her to you as a helper, a partner.

ADAM: Oh, is this the arm and a leg deal? *(Looks down at appendages in relief)*

GOD: No, It's the rib deal.

ADAM: Oh, okay. What does that include from the original list?

GOD: You'll find out.

ADAM: What am I supposed to do with her?

GOD: Go forth, be fruitful and multiply.

ADAM: Fruit, I love fruit! Thanks for the addition *(Looks at Eve)* Sorry you had to subtract some things. I suppose now I will have to divide things equally. But multiply, what's that?

GOD: You'll figure it out!

ADAM: Well, let's take a look at you. Where I am smooth, you are, well, lumpy.

EVE: And where I am smooth, you are...

GOD: I don't give anatomy lessons. Would you like a copy of the Kinsey Report? You'll figure it out.

EVE: Adam, why don't you show me around the Garden.

ADAM: Sure, come on and I'll give you a tour. These are all the plants and trees God gave me to use and enjoy. I named them all.

EVE: Can you wait a minute. Is there a restroom?

ADAM: A what?

EVE: Never mind. I'll just find a spot behind this bush. And then I am going out to look for some apparel!

ADAM: A pear. Great! I like pears!

EVE: Adam, it's fashion, not fruit!

(EVE *lowers head to indicate leaving.*)

GOD: So, how's it going, Adam?

ADAM: God, she is a real pain. I liked the peace and quiet in the garden before she showed up. She talks too much. She'll tell me what to do. She'll want to change me. What is taking her so long?

GOD: I gave her to you to teach you patience.

ADAM: Okay, but tell me again why you created her.

GOD: All the reasons I shared with you before. But really, it was because I was afraid you would get lost in the Garden and would not ask for directions.

EVE: I'm back and I have a fashion show for you. I found lots of leaves and will start with these three possibilities. First, an ivy. Nice contours, lacy edging, and a sumptuous green.

ADAM: Great! But it is Poison Ivy. Probably don't want to sit on that!

EVE: Well, here's the next one. Does this make my backside look too big?

ADAM: It's not called an Elephant Ear for nothing!

EVE: *(Starts crying)*

ADAM: What are you doing? You're spilling water all over the place! You know you are the only woman for me!

EVE: You think I look fat. And old. And like I haven't slept for a week. *(More tears)* I need a compliment.

ADAM: *(Stumbling over the words)* Well...your eyesight is perfect.

GOD: Adam, you are not scoring any points.

ADAM: *(to Eve)* I don't have a fig of a notion why you are acting like a waterfall.

EVE: *(Looks up to Adam and greets him with a big smile)* Oh, thank you, Adam. The fig leaf was my first choice too. Let's get ready for a date night.

ADAM: Let's continue our tour of the Garden. I called this one a palm tree.

EVE: Its leaves are kind of prickly. I would have called it a blade tree.

ADAM: This one I called a pine tree.

EVE: It's covered with long spiky things. I would have called it a needle tree.

ADAM: This one I named an oak tree.

EVE: It's covered with little brown things that fall to the ground. I would have called it a nut tree.

ADAM: *(To God)* This new partner you gave me is sort of, well, you know...she has a mind of her own.

EVE: What is this tree?

ADAM: I call it an apple tree.

EVE: It looks good. I want to pick one and taste it.

GOD: Oh, no, you don't. This is my tree and it is the only one in the Garden you may not touch.

EVE: What happens if I touch it?

GOD: If you touch it you will die.

EVE: What does it mean to die?

GOD: Touch that tree and you'll find out.

EVE: Hmmm. Well, if you say so. Adam, What are these creatures who have gathered around us in the garden?

ADAM: Those are called animals. God gave them all to me to enjoy and I named every one of them. This one is called a rhinoceros. That one over by the stream is called an elephant. And I named that tall one a giraffe. Over there by the waterfall is a hippopotamus.

EVE: What hard names you gave these poor creatures. Couldn't you have found easier names for them?

ADAM: Are you always going to be so difficult?

EVE: I am very easy to get along with. In the future you might ask me before you make big decisions like naming everything.

ADAM: God, she's sort of bossy. Can I give her back?

GOD: You'll figure her out.

EVE: *(Studying Adam's hair)* Adam, your hair is a mess. How long has it been since you have had a haircut?

ADAM: A what?

EVE: It could be a little shorter around the ears. I like the wave at the top, but it needs to be parted. The back doesn't look bad, just a little layering would help.

ADAM: No one touches my hair, thank you.

EVE: We'll discuss it later. By the way, where do we sleep?

ADAM: I made a nice clearing under the oak tree for resting and sleeping.

EVE: You mean under the tree with those hard little brown things falling day and night?

ADAM: It works for me.

EVE: I'll help you gather some wood and leaves and you can make us a little shelter. It should have three rooms.

ADAM: Three rooms? Whatever for?

EVE: One for me and one for you for sleeping and one for just hanging out.

GOD: That wasn't what I had in mind when I created you.

EVE: We'll work that out later. And you can make some furniture. We'll need a table and two chairs for eating. I may want to bring in some supplies so you can make a cupboard to set near the table.

ADAM: Wait a minute. We don't work in the garden. No toiling, no sweating, no pressure. Everything we need is furnished.

EVE: Now don't complain Adam. We can always improve upon things.

ADAM: God, Is she always so demanding?

GOD: I gave her to you. You can work it out.

EVE: Now, we'll need a roof over our dwelling. Maybe you could string vines across the top and cover them with those great big leaves. What did you name them?

ADAM: Elephant ears.

EVE: No, no. Not the elephant's ears. Those great big leaves.

ADAM: Those great big leaves are called "Elephant's ears."

EVE: Perhaps you could have been more creative. Were you running out of names and started to use the same ones over again? It's too bad I wasn't around when the naming was going on. I have all kinds of ideas. Have you already named the birds and the crawling things? I could help with those. I could help with naming the flowers too. There are so many beautiful ones.

ADAM: All done naming everything. God, does she always talk so much?

GOD: Humor her. You will come to love her.

ADAM: Love her? I don't even understand her.

GOD: Believe me, you can love her without understanding her.

EVE: Now we should get organized. Let's make a schedule. On the first day of the week we will clean the dwelling. I'll tidy up and you sweep the floor. On the second day of the week I can construct some clothing for us. Do you prefer boxers or briefs?

ADAM: Good heavens, partner. We don't work in the garden. And we don't need clothes.

EVE: I could weave a cute little skirt out of those small vines. And those big leaves would make a darling hat. Adam, if you would gather some of those flowers I could make a lei to hang around my neck.

ADAM: Not necessary. *(Studying Eve)* I like you the way you are.

EVE: Thank you. Now, on the third, fifth, and sixth day of the week we can bathe. I'll make soap so we can lather up and clean off the grime. The waterfall should make a nice shower for us.

ADAM: You forgot the fourth day. Surely you have plans for the fourth day.

EVE: Certainly, on the fourth day we will plan trips. How big is the Garden? We can explore a different part each week.

ADAM: Woman, you are exhausting me just thinking about it. We don't need a schedule. In the garden we just relax and enjoy.

EVE: But that will get boring. Busy hands will keep us out of trouble.

ADAM: What sort of trouble could we possibly get into in this perfect place?

GOD: Didn't I already tell you?

EVE: And on the seventh day, we shall rest. Just like God did after he created the world.

ADAM: What is your definition of resting?

EVE: Do you know any games? We can play games. We can make up games or I can teach you some. God gave me a very creative mind and I would be glad to share all my talents with you.

ADAM: I know a game we can play. I run across a field carrying a coconut and you try to take it from me. If I reach the end of the field with the coconut I get six points. Then I get to kick the coconut over a post at the end of the field and if I am successful I get another point. We can call it "football."

EVE: What a silly idea. Who would ever invent such a game?

ADAM: You'd be surprised!

EVE: Or we can just carry on a conversation. You can tell me all about your life before I came into the garden and all your plans for the future.

ADAM: My plans were to rest and enjoy the garden in peace.

EVE: I wonder why God won't let us touch that tree in the center of the garden? I'd like to taste those red things hanging on the tree?

ADAM: I called them apples.

EVE: Well, I can't see why we can't just pick a few apples. What harm can it be?

ADAM: God said, "No" so leave it be woman. Pick your apples from any other tree.

EVE: But the creature you named serpent said that if we eat of the fruit from God's tree we will not die. Instead, our eyes will be opened and we will be like God and know the difference between good and evil.

ADAM: Leave it be, woman. We do not touch that tree.

EVE: What harm can there be in getting smarter? I don't know what "evil" means but maybe we should find out. Where is God now? He isn't anywhere around and will never know we touched his tree.

ADAM: Woman, you are trying my patience. Don't touch that tree.

EVE: All right Adam, You win. I guess we'll never know what would have happened if we would have touched that tree.

ADAM: Let's go work on that football game. You find a coconut and I'll build the goal posts.

EVE: Yes, dear. *(Aside)* He finally figured it out. I'm a keeper.

Forty Days and Forty Nights

by Jean Mosby

CAST:

NOAH
NOAH'S WIFE

SCENE: Morning, as Noah and his wife awaken on the Ark

WIFE: Noah! The rooster is crowing. Wake up!

NOAH: Good morning, dear. Is it still raining?

WIFE: Yes, pouring. Just like it has been for nearly six weeks.

NOAH: And did you sleep well?

WIFE: Sleep well! The sheep were bleating beneath us. The lions were roaring above us...and you snored all night.

NOAH: I do not snore.

WIFE: You snored enough to shake the rafters of the Ark.

NOAH: That must have been the elephants on the first floor.

WIFE: Not a chance.

NOAH: The snakes are getting out of hand. I told them to "Go forth and multiply."

WIFE: Noah, you know they can't multiply. They are adders.

NOAH: I got cold during the night but a warm, fuzzy kitten crawled into bed and snuggled up beside me.

WIFE: That warm, fuzzy kitten was a skunk.

NOAH: Oh, dear.

WIFE: I shooed him away. Then I got up during the night for a cup of warm milk and found a mouse in the kitchen.

NOAH: A mouse in the kitchen!

WIFE: Yes, I chased him with a broom but the little bugger got away.

NOAH: Now, dear, you know we must not harm anyone. There must be two of everything.

WIFE: Well, you find him and put him in his cage or next time he will meet his maker.

NOAH: I'll take care of it.

WIFE: By the way, when I went to get milk there wasn't any. Our son Ham's wife is in charge of the milking. Is she doing her job?

NOAH: Yes, but she tells me neither Elsie or Daisy are producing lately.

WIFE: I guess they are producing Milk Duds.

NOAH: I will talk to Elsie and Daisy.

WIFE: Thank you dear. Hopefully your encouragement will go in one ear and out the udder.

NOAH: I am starving. Would you fix me an omelet for breakfast?

WIFE: There will be no omelet this morning. Our son Shem stopped by earlier to say that the foxes got into the hen coop and ate all the eggs.

NOAH: Well what else do we have?

WIFE: I can fix you a piece of toast. Would you like butter?

NOAH: Yes, but where did you get the butter?

WIFE: The Ark rocked so bad in the storm that the cream turned to butter.

NOAH: Yes, it was a rough night.

WIFE: Some day the rain will stop and the Ark will land.

NOAH: It could land on a nice, flat plain.

WIFE: Or it could land on the top of a mountain.

NOAH: Oh, I doubt that.

WIFE: If we land on the top of a mountain it could be cold. I have not packed cold-weather clothes.

NOAH: What could we do then?

WIFE: I am going to make myself a fur coat.

NOAH: Where will you get the fur?

WIFE: Don't even ask.

NOAH: We could land on a sandy beach.

WIFE: I didn't pack any sun-tan lotion. By the way, what happened this afternoon? You were out on the deck for hours fishing and you came back with nothing.

NOAH: For crying out loud, you have the memory of a gnat. You know I had only two worms.

WIFE: By the way, the carrier pigeon had something in his craw today.

NOAH: What was he complaining about today?

WIFE: No, he literally had something in his craw. I pulled it out. It was a note, a little messy, but readable.

NOAH: Well, what did it say?

WIFE: *(Reading)* Dear Noah, We could have sworn you said we were leaving at 4:00. Sincerely, the Unicorns.

NOAH: So that's why they got left behind.

WIFE: Our son Shem reports that some of the animals are not happy.

NOAH: Complain, complain, complain. That's all these animals do.

WIFE: Yes, the aardvark stopped me today and complained, "You brought only two ants?"

NOAH: The elephants are complaining about lack of space.

WIFE: No wonder. They overpacked. They brought two trunks.

NOAH: Indeed!

WIFE: Well at least the roosters listened when you told everyone to pack light.

NOAH: Yes, they brought only their combs.

WIFE: And the horses are pessimistic. They say "Neigh" to everything I ask them to do.

NOAH: And you just can't trust some of them.

WIFE: Who can't you trust?

NOAH: The Cheetahs. No more Texas Hold'em for them.

WIFE: Noah, dear, I haven't seen two dinosaurs. Didn't they board the ark as you told them to do?

NOAH: No, sadly they refused. They got a good deal on a cruise ship.

WIFE: I know it has been a lot of work to get this ark built and afloat.

NOAH: Yes, I sent the specs for the ark to the city and it took two months to get approval of the building code.

WIFE: Then the neighbors objected that you were violating the zoning ordinances by building the ark in the front yard so you had to get a variance from the city planning board.

NOAH: Then I had a problem getting the wood for the ark because there was a ban on cutting trees.

WIFE: You finally got permission from the environmentalists since you were saving two spotted owls.

NOAH: Then the rains came and the whole world was in liquidation.

WIFE: And what a good investor you turned out to be when you decided to float your stock.

NOAH: Yes, I raised a lot of capital just before the market sank.

NOAH: How are the boys and their wives getting along on the Ark?

WIFE: Well, I worry a little bit about our son Japheth's new wife. They were married such a short time before the rains began.

NOAH: It hasn't been much of a honeymoon I suppose.

WIFE: He did promise her a cruise.

NOAH: I put them in a nice room on the third floor.

WIFE: It's not exactly a room with a view. All they see is water.

NOAH: And what of Ham and his wife?

WIFE: Too bad she gets so seasick.

NOAH: Especially in the morning.

WIFE: You don't suppose?

NOAH: Might it be?

WIFE: Our first grandchild?

NOAH: God did say, "Be fruitful and multiply."

WIFE: Yes, we will have to repopulate the earth.

NOAH: Well don't look at me. I'm six hundred years old.

WIFE: That's why God invented those little blue pills.

NOAH: Let's leave the repopulating to our kids.

WIFE: As you always say, "With God anything is possible."

NOAH: Do you hear that?

WIFE: What?

NOAH: That buzzing sound. It sounds like…like…bees. Did you find a safe place for them where I could easily find them?

WIFE: Yes, of course. Where else? They are in the Ark hives.

NOAH: How are Shem and his wife doing?

WIFE: They seem like a happy couple.

NOAH: Yes, she finally got her wish. A trip to the zoo.

WIFE: And a new job as the zookeeper's wife.

NOAH: Is Ham getting along with his wife?

WIFE: I believe so. He chose a rather precocious little gal.

NOAH: Yes, she is a courageous little thing.

WIFE: Maybe you could put her at taming those lions.

NOAH: Speaking of lions, have the boys reported on the animals this morning?

WIFE: Ham said one of the giraffes has a neck ache.

NOAH: I'll have to get out the ladder and give him an adjustment.

WIFE: And the hippopotamuses are passing a lot of gas.

NOAH: No wonder it has been so noisy down below. I'll have to change their diet.

WIFE: Well, do it fast. The monkeys are all moving up to the second floor.

NOAH: Yes, dear.

WIFE: Shem chased the kangaroos from the pantry last evening.

NOAH: Yes, they were raiding the vegetable bin.

WIFE: The peacocks and swans were arguing yesterday over who is the most beautiful.

NOAH: Shem's wife decided to stage a beauty contest for them. They are both preening for the contest next week.

WIFE: I haven't seen the panda bears lately.

NOAH: Ham found them snuggling in the hay loft.

WIFE: Jepheth said the rabbits are overrunning the Ark. Can you do something?

NOAH: But there were just two rabbits when we started.

WIFE: Do they have to be so fruitful?

NOAH: Who's cooking tonight?

WIFE: Japheth's wife.

NOAH: I'll tell her we'll have rabbit stew.

WIFE: Now what? The lights are out.

NOAH: The eels are refusing to work. I must set up some flood lights. *(Laughs at his own joke)* Get it? FLOOD lights.

WIFE: *(Groans)*

NOAH: How are things in the kitchen, dear?

WIFE: You'll have to do something about the loggerhead turtles.

NOAH: What's the problem?

WIFE: They couldn't find any sand so they laid their eggs in the flour bins.

NOAH: Did Ham tell you that the bulls wasted no time introducing themselves to the cows?

WIFE: I heard one of them is expecting a calf already.

NOAH: She might be. She's getting a little goofy. Yesterday I caught her saying to a block of cheese, "Don't you know I'm your mother."

WIFE: By the way, Noah, what are you doing with the animal waste that accumulates?

NOAH: I told Shem to throw it out the window into the waters.

WIFE: I hope the EPA doesn't hear about this.

NOAH: Mum's the word.

WIFE: By the way, the odor coming from the elephant pen hasn't been so bad. What are you doing with their "droppings?"

NOAH: I told Shem to back them up against an open window whenever they need to "go" and the rain washes their behinds.

WIFE: Oh, sort of like a bidet.

NOAH: You could call it that.

WIFE: In your spare time can you fix the kitchen table?

NOAH: What's wrong with the kitchen table?

WIFE: The goats have eaten one of the legs.

NOAH: Well, then I'd better get going. I'll start on the table leg first.

WIFE: While you are doing that I am going to take a shower.

NOAH: We don't have a shower.

WIFE: We do now. The roof leaks.

NOAH: I'll put that on my honey-do list.

WIFE: And another thing that needs attention...

NOAH: Wife, do you hear the quiet?

WIFE: What quiet?

NOAH: The pounding rain stopped for the first time in forty days.

WIFE: You are right! Call the boys and their wives! This is so exciting!

NOAH: Quiet, woman, God is talking to me.

WIFE: What is he saying?

NOAH: Throw open the shutters and look outside.

WIFE: The storm is over. The sun is shining. Oh, Noah, come and see the arc of color spreading across the sky.

NOAH: What a wonderful sign of promise and of hope and of new beginnings.

Samson and Delilah

by Jean Mosby

CAST:

SAMSON, wearing a wig of long, curly, dark hair and an overshirt depicting bare chest and oversized muscles.
DELILAH, highly made up, wearing attractive clothing and jewelry.

SAMSON: I am thankful I am the best looking male in all of Israel. Why, my long, flowing curls are the envy of all the court. Not only that, I am considered "eye candy" by all the women in the land. My strength is unequaled in all the land. *(Flexes his muscles)* Not one soul knows that my strength comes from my beautiful, long hair. *(Flips his curls)* God considers me special, which I certainly am. He has personally chosen me to begin the breaking of the Philistine's forty-year rule over Israel.

DELILAH: *(Aside)* I am the beautiful, seductive and cunning Delilah. I am at the door of the amazing, awesome, gorgeous, but conceited Samson. I have been hired by the lords of the Philistines to seduce him in order to learn the secret of his strength. The Philistines fear Samson, but cannot apprehend him until they know the secret of his strength. As you can see, I am no slouch myself.

(Knock, knock)

SAMSON: Who is there?

DELILAH: Pizza delivery.

SAMSON: Come right in.

DELILAH: Hi, It's Delilah.

SAMSON: No pizza?

DELILAH: No pizza. How else could I get to spend time with the most gorgeous, smartest, muscular man in all of Israel?

SAMSON: *(Preening)* Well, do come in Delilah. Yes, I am the most gorgeous, smartest, muscular man in all of Israel. Do have a seat in this fine chair where you can admire me from the best angle.

DELILAH: *(Leaning in to Samson)* Why thank you but I believe I can admire you better from this angle, so I will sit beside you here on the edge of your couch.

SAMSON: Fine, I do believe my left side is my best profile.

DELILAH: *(Stroking Samson's arm)* My what muscles you have. Why they ripple like a bubbling brook running over the stones in the stream.

SAMSON: They do, indeed.

DELILAH: Do you use performance enhancing drugs?

SAMSON: *(Shocked)* I beg your pardon!

DELILAH: You know. Steroids for muscle growth. Is that the secret of your strength?

SAMSON: No way. I keep a membership at the health club down the road. Did you know I can bench press two hundred pounds. For my weight, that is the advanced level. Really builds these biceps. *(Flexes the upper arm muscles)*

DELILAH: Oh, be still my beating heart!

SAMSON: In addition to the bench press, each day I spend half an hour on the rowing machine. Really strengthens my abs. *(He strokes his tummy muscles.)*

DELILAH: *(Panting)* May I come and watch sometime?

SAMSON: Sorry, women are not allowed. After the rowing machine I work out for half an hour on the Elliptical Machine. Really strengthens my pectorals. *(Beats on chest)*

DELILAH: *(Gasping)* The thought of it gives me goosebumps!

SAMSON: I finish up with half an hour on the Monster Lat Pulldown Machine to strengthen the glutes.

DELILAH: And where are the glutes?

SAMSON: The glutes are the largest muscles in the body. They are the muscles in the buttocks.

DELILAH: *(Fanning herself)* Do tell! And your muscles are so beautifully tanned.

SAMSON: Thirty minutes a day lounging on the rooftop on sunny days. On rainy days I catch my rays at the tanning salon.

DELILAH: You have quite a reputation for doing amazing feats of strength.

SAMSON: Oh, everyone has heard of my strength. Why I tore apart a lion with my bare hands. *(Growling and tearing with his hands)*

DELILAH: *(Swooning)* How manly of you. How did that happen?

SAMSON: I wanted to marry a Philistine woman, and when I went down to Timnah with my parents to meet her, a young lion attacked me in the vineyards and I killed him. Just like that.

DELILAH: *(Stroking his arms)* Just like that! Oh, it's too much for a woman to bear. But you say you wanted to marry a Philistine woman. What did your parents have to say about that?

SAMSON: Well, they weren't very happy about me marrying outside my faith, but they eventually agreed.

DELILAH: So, was this woman as beautiful as me?

SAMSON: That is a loaded question.

DELILAH: Did she have my skin, which is as warm and luscious as an olive?

SAMSON: I am taking the fifth on that one.

DELILAH: Were her cheeks glowing as pink and delicious as mine?

SAMSON: *(Pondering)* No, they were more copper-colored I think.

DELILAH: *(Pouting)* Well, then, were her arms as long and graceful as mine?

SAMSON: Again, I'm taking the fifth on that one.

DELILAH: Were her words sweet as honey, like mine?

SAMSON: The fifth.

DELILAH: Her words? When she asked you the secret of your strength, what did you answer?

SAMSON: The secret of my strength? Why, I refused to tell her.

DELILAH: Oh, drat!

SAMSON: Watch your language. You are speaking to a man of God.

DELILAH: Yes, dear. Tell me more about your wedding to this not-as-beautiful-as-me Philistine woman.

SAMSON: Yes, there's more. When I returned to wed her I passed by the lion's carcass and there was a swarm of bees in the carcass and a honeycomb full of sweet honey.

DELILAH: And did you marry this not-as-beautiful-as-me Philistine woman?

SAMSON: Yes, I did marry the maybe-not-so-beautiful-as you woman.

DELILAH: *(Looking triumphant)* There, you admitted that I am more beautiful than your bride. Glory, hallelujah!

SAMSON: Now, I didn't exactly say that.

DELILAH: Yes, yes, you did! Well, anyway, go on. You married the not-as-beautiful-as-me woman.

SAMSON: After the wedding we had a huge wedding feast and I asked this riddle: Out of the eater came something to eat. Out of the strong came something sweet.

DELILAH: Could the men at the feast answer the riddle? Did they know the answer was the lion and honey?

SAMSON: They did not know the answer for three days.

DELILAH: Well, did they get the answer to your riddle on the fourth day?

SAMSON: On the fourth day they nagged my wife to coax the answer from me and she did.

DELILAH: Oh, so you can be coaxed to give out an answer to a question? I must learn from this not-so-beautiful-as-me wife of yours.

SAMSON: This certainly-not-as-beautiful-as-you wife of mine had to be unfaithful to me in order to tell them the answer to my riddle.

DELILAH: There, you said it again! I am more beautiful than your Philistine wife.

SAMSON: Well, yes, Delilah you are more beautiful than my unfaithful, scheming, intolerable wife.

DELILAH: Oh, Samson, my dear, thank you for the compliment, even though it was hard-gotten. Go on, then, what happened next.

SAMSON: I became so jealous that I killed thirty men and my father was so angry with me that he gave my wife away to my friend. Can you believe!

DELILAH: So you are no longer married to the not-so-beautiful-as-me wife?

SAMSON: No, but when I wanted to go in with my wife anyway, I was not allowed to enter her quarters and I got really, really mad.

DELILAH: Of course you did. What did your dad do then?

SAMSON: My dad sent me to an anger management class.

DELILAH: How dare anyone oppose the mighty Samson?

SAMSON: Right! But I am not just strong. I am very clever. Oh, I am so smart! I set fire to the tails of three hundred foxes and set them loose in the fields of the Philistines. Burned up all their grain, vineyards, and olive groves in Judah. Oh, you should have seen!

DELILAH: Yes, I heard that PETA brought a lawsuit against you for harming all those foxes.

SAMSON: Yes, they did, but the lawsuit was dismissed because, as you know, I have been a judge in Israel for twenty years and the case came to my court.

DELILAH: Oh, Sampson, you are so important in all the land. But you are best known for your strength. How do you come by all this strength? Surely you can tell me, the more-beautiful-than-your-exwife woman?

SAMPSON: I could not tell her and I cannot tell you the source of my strength, no matter how beautiful you are.

DELILAH: *(Exasperated)* Oh, pickles. Foiled again.

SAMPSON: Please do not use that language around me, a man of God.

DELILAH: Sorry for the language. So, were the Philistines really angry with you after you burned their grain, vineyards, and olive groves in Judah?

SAMPSON: Yes, when I came to Lehi the Philistines came after me.

DELILAH: Is that when you killed the thousand men?

SAMPSON: Yes it was. I picked up the jawbone of a donkey that was lying around and with it I slew a thousand men. Guess I showed those Philistines. These muscles never fail me.

DELILAH: I'd be happy to massage those muscles for you.

SAMSON: Deep tissue or Swedish?

DELILAH: You'll find I am well trained to do both. To what do you attribute your extraordinary strength?

SAMSON: *(Winking)* That is for me to know and you to find out.

DELILAH: I have an idea. Let's play riddles.

SAMSON: OK. I love riddles.

DELILAH: Here's one for you. I weigh nothing, but you can still see me. If you put me in a bucket, I make the bucket lighter. What am I?

SAMSON: Hmmm. Weigh nothing. Still see me. Put in a bucket. Make bucket lighter. I give up.

DELILAH: A hole, silly.

SAMSON: Of course. Now it's my turn. I fell off a 20-foot ladder. I wasn't hurt. How come?

DELILAH: You fell in the water? You fell in some bushes?

SAMSON: *(Shaking his head at her answers)* I fell off the bottom step.

DELILAH: *(Laughing)* I'll get you on this one. What has a foot on each side and one in the middle?

SAMSON: *(Pondering)* Hmmm. A foot on each side and one in the middle? I know. A monster!

DELILAH: No, not a monster. A yardstick.

SAMSON: Oh, of course. A yardstick.

DELILAH: One more riddle. What is the source of your strength?

SAMSON: I know that one. My...oh, no you don't. I told you three times already about ways you can take away my strength.

DELILAH: Yes, the first time you said if I would bind you with seven fresh bowstrings you would lose your strength.

SAMSON: And you tried it while I slept and it didn't work. I woke up and broke the bowstrings.

DELILAH: You shouldn't play games with me Samson. Do you have any idea how much I had to pay for seven fresh bowstrings that didn't even work?

SAMSON: *(Smugly)* Not my problem.

DELILAH: And the second time I asked you for the source of your strength you told me to bind you with new ropes while you slept.

SAMSON: Right. And it didn't work. *(Smirking)* But you sure had fun trying.

DELILAH: Do you have any idea how much effort it was to haul seven new ropes over here? What a waste of effort when they didn't work.

SAMSON: Poor Delilah!

DELILAH: And the third time I asked you for the source of your strength you told me to weave seven locks of your head and make it tight with a pin.

SAMSON: Which you did and I got a smart new hair style. But it didn't work for you, did it?

DELILAH: Speaking of hair styles, *(Twirling a lock around her finger)* how ever do you keep your hair so shiny?

SAMSON: My secret is an olive oil cream rinse. It's a special formula I picked up down at the marketplace.

DELILAH: Is your hair naturally curly?

SAMSON: Well, just between you and me, I have it done at the salon each week.

DELILAH: Rollers or hot comb?

SAMSON: Rollers. I wouldn't put a hot comb to my hair. Too drying.

DELILAH: Is this your natural hair color?

SAMSON: Yes, the beautiful chestnut color is natural. However, I must admit to a touch of gold highlights.

DELILAH: L'Oreal or Madison Reed hair color brand for the highlights?

SAMSON: Oh, I wouldn't put anything on my beautiful hair but L-Oreal. Have you seen their latest Henna shade? Do you think I ought to try it?

DELILAH: Well, personally, I can't see you in Henna. Maybe a light ash blond.

SAMSON: Perhaps you are right. I have heard that blondes have more fun.

DELILAH: What do you do for fun Samson?

SAMSON: I'm training for the discus throw. I'm hoping to qualify for the Olympics.

DELILAH: Have you been to Greece before?

SAMSON: Certainly. I went to the Olympics eight years ago to compete in the slingshot event.

DELILAH: I love the slingshot event. Tell me about it.

SAMPSON: *(Excitedly)* I used a twenty-pound sling, attached to a foot-high fork of strong oak. I picked up a round ten-pound rock, set it into my sling, took a firm stance, pulled back the sling, released the sling and the rock went flying into the air and landed with a thud thirty feet away. The crowd stood up and roared their admiration.

DELILAH: I'll bet you took home the gold medal.

SAMSON: No, just the silver. Some puny little shepherd guy named David shot a rock thirty-five feet. Took away my thunderous reception.

DELILAH: Do they have a donkey's jawbone tossing event? With your experience, I'd wager that you would get the gold.

SAMSON: True, true. I am the greatest at that. Sadly, there is no donkey jawbone tossing event at the Olympics.

DELILAH: Now, my dear, I would like to ask you a personal question.

SAMSON: You ask a lot of questions. I am tired of your questions.

DELILAH: *(Aside)* I am getting nowhere at learning the source of his strength. Let me try a different approach. If I get him drunk he might reveal the source of his strength. *(Hauls out a bottle of wine from her bag)*

SAMSON: What's that?

DELILAH: Shiloh Shor Cabernet Sauvignon, the finest wine one can buy.

SAMSON: Sorry. I cannot drink wine.

DELILAH: But this wine is noted for its deep fruity flavor. Imported from Italy. Vintage 1120 B.C. Thirty-five shekels a bottle.

SAMSON: Sorry, I am a nazarite. I am forbidden to drink wine.

DELILAH: Oh, fiddlesticks.

SAMSON: Watch your language.

DELILAH: *(Reaching into her bag again)* I have brought you a delicious snack. Have one of these.

SAMSON: I am a nazarite. I can't eat that.

DELILAH: Well, what can you eat?

SAMSON: Honey.

DELILAH: How sweet of you to call me Honey.

SAMSON: I am not calling you Honey.

DELILAH: But you just called me Honey.

SAMSON: You asked me what I can eat and I told you honey.

DELILAH: I would like to be your honey.

SAMSON: Why would you like to be my honey?

DELILAH: Because honeys share secrets with each other. They don't withhold anything from their beloved.

SAMSON: Not anything?

DELILAH: Not anything.

SAMSON: All right. You can be my honey. What is it you would like to know?

DELILAH: What is the secret of your strength?

SAMSON: The secret of my strength? Hmmm. *(Pondering)* If I tell you, do you promise not to tell anyone else? Ever!

DELILAH: Cross my heart and hope to die. You can trust me.

SAMSON: All right, if you promise. The secret of my strength lies in my beautiful, highlighted, curly, chestnut-colored hair.

DELILAH: Your hair!

SAMSON: That's right. My head has never been shaved. If a razor ever touches my head I will be weak.

DELILAH: Samson, dear, I have to be running. It was great to see you again.

SAMSON: But you just got here!

DELILAH: By, dear.

SAMSON: See you soon, Delilah.

DELILAH: *(Aside)* Oh, how the mighty will fall! At last I know the secret of Samson's strength. I will give this information to the Philistines and collect my eleven hundred pieces of silver....Unlike Samson... I am Woman. I am invincible. *(Can be said or sung)*

Jonah and the Whale

A Readers' Theater Monologue

by Jean Mosby

Hi, I'm Jonah. You probably heard that I had an encounter with a whale. Did I ever! In fact, there's a whole book in the Bible about me and that whale. My book is hard to find because I rated just barely over two pages and I'm stuck between two other guys you probably never heard of, Obadiah and Micah. Well, here's my story straight from the horse's mouth.

There I was, relaxing in my recliner having a cigar, when I heard this thunderous voice saying, "Jonah, this is God speaking. Get off your butt and go at once to Nineveh and tell the king and all his people they have to repent of their wickedness or I will destroy them."

Now, I ain't no sissy, but this is a tall order. Nineveh is a city of 127,000 and they are all as mean as a bed of rattlesnakes. They don't know the meaning of the word "repent," and they'll tear me limb from limb when they hear my message. So I did what any ordinary guy would do. I ran in the opposite direction. Figured God would find some other guy to reform Nineveh.

Now where would a guy go to hide from God? I pictured myself floatin' down the Nile, maybe catchin' sight of a few pyramids. Or how about a trip to Italy. Can't you see me being rowed down a canal while a gondolier strums Italian melodies? But no, where did I decide to go? The city of Tarshish, Greece, about as far from Nineveh as I could get.

So I went down to Joppa and found a ship headed for Tarshish. Now, God got pretty mad at me for disobeying him and caused a bad storm to come up while we're out there in the middle of the sea. And let me tell you, when God is angry, he can whip up one terrible, awful storm. The waves were so strong the sailors were afraid the ship would break up. It didn't help when the sailors threw the cargo overboard to lighten the ship. What a shame to waste all those cases of rum.

Now, all this time I'm sleeping down in the hold of the ship. Let me tell you, once I fall asleep ain't no storm on earth gonna wake me up. Well, God had other plans. The crew was so afraid of my God they decided it was my fault they were about to drown, so they thought it best to throw me overboard.

Suddenly I'm ripped from my hammock in a sound sleep, dragged to the deck, and splash, I land in the tumultuous briney. And God immediately calms the sea. This makes the sailors happy but I'm not in such a good position here. Did I mention that I can't swim?

As I'm flailing and splashing, about to drown, along comes this huge open mouth and swallows me whole. I slide down a long tongue into a vast darkness. Hauling out my cell phone and clicking on the light, I start checking out my surroundings. This is no picnic, as the darn beast keeps slapping that wide tail against the water's surface, which tosses me against his rib cage every time. Who ever named this guy a "gentle giant?"

This guy is no "Nemo." He has a case of bad breath that a carton of mints wouldn't solve. After three days and three nights I tell God I'm sorry for disobeying. And suddenly, woosh! I am spewed out like Toto in a hurricane. Right onto dry land.

Now, God doesn't save me without exacting a price. He says, "This time when I say that you should go to Nineveh, you go." And that's how I ended up in Nineveh. But that's another story.

The Extended Warranty Call

A 2-minute Comedy Skit

by Jean Mosby

CAST:

ANDREA: A telemarketer
LISA: A lonely housewife

LISA: *(Picking up phone)* Hello.

ANDREA: This is Andrea on a recorded line. How are you doing today?

LISA: Oh, Andrea, you wouldn't believe the day I have had! I barely got out of bed when I tripped over the cat. Fluffy is such a darling cat but so easily gets under foot. I went down so fast and landed on poor Fluffy. She was OK but I think I sprained my ankle.

ANGIE: I am glad you are OK. I am calling about your auto warranty which is about to expire.

LISA: Well, Andrea, would you believe it? Last night I left my headlights on while I was at Myrtle's house for our weekly bridge night and I ran down the battery. I had to call Triple A and get a tow. They are putting in a new battery as we speak.

ANDREA: How old is your car?

LISA: How old is our car? Not enough to trade in for a new one. My husband Fred and I had an argument last week. He wants to trade in my beautiful little car for an electric car. Angie, do you know what I paid to fill my tank last week? $4.90 a gallon.

ANDREA: I am calling about extending your...

THE EXTENDED WARRANTY CALL

LISA: $4.90 a gallon! Where is our country headed with gas prices like that? It's enough to cancel our vacation this summer. Have you ever been to Lake Tahoe? We were planning to go to a lodge there for a wonderful week, but Fred says we have to plan a staycation instead.

ANDREA: You could save a lot of money with our extended...

LISA: Did I mention that my brother-in-law Harold and his wife Mae wanted to come along to Lake Tahoe. What a vacation that would have been. Mae can talk your ear off. I can never get a word in edgewise. Well, I put a damper on that one fast.

ANDREA: Ahem...

LISA: Mae is such a terrible gossip. She is a terrible cook. Oh, the things I could tell you about her. At the last church potluck she brought jello with canned fruit in it. Jello! After I slaved away for two hours preparing a beef pot roast with mushroom gravy.

ANDREA: About the extended warranty...

LISA: Speaking of pot roast. Would you like my recipe Andrea? It won first place at the county fair in 1983. There is a secret ingredient which I never share. But I feel like I can trust you not to share with anyone else. You'd be surprised what a half cup of whiskey can add to that mushroom gravy. Why, the judges ate three servings before they declared me the winner.

ANDREA: How many miles do you drive your car in a ...

LISA: Well, Andrea, that depends. Did I tell you Fred fell off a ladder last July? Yes, he did. He broke his leg and I had to drive back and forth to the hospital for two weeks. I told him to hire someone to clean out the gutters, but you know these men. Are you married Andrea?

ANDREA: I am single. Now about that extended warranty...

LISA: Oh, you poor thing. Was it a divorce? Did the love of your life pass away? Were you jilted at the altar? Well, don't you fret about it dear. My advice to you is to get out more. Have you tried one of the internet dating services? Do be careful though. There are a lot of kooky people out there.

ANDREA: The advantages of our extended warranty are...

LISA: I have a great idea Andrea. My brother is single too. He can call you at this number, or would you prefer he call at home? He is quite good looking and...

HELLO, Andrea, are you there? Too bad, we got disconnected.

The Old Woman Who Lived in a Shoe

In Her Defense

by Jean Mosby

CAST:

NARRATOR
OLD WOMAN

NARRATOR:

There was an old woman who lived in a shoe,
She had so many children she didn't know what to do.
She gave them some broth without any bread,
And whipped them all soundly and put them to bed.

For years we all have been reading and sharing with the kids the nursery rhyme, "The Old Woman in the Shoe". I have to tell you I had some reservations about this old woman.

Why did that woman have so many children? Not that it's my business, but it did raise some questions for me. If she didn't know what to do with them, why did she...well, as I said, not my business. She gave the children broth for dinner? And...no bread! and she whipped them and put them to bed! I see you are just as outraged as I was.

I met her the other day, and as Paul Harvey used to say, Here's the rest of the story.

JEAN MOSBY

THE OLD WOMAN:

Hey, I am that old woman. Some silly old goose wrote that rhyme about me away back when. Gave me a bit of a bad rap. Now, in my defense, I'm gonna set you straight on a couple of things.

About the shoe thing. It is a pretty neat shoe. Actually a pretty classy ladies boot, laced all the way to the top. Four floors, actually, so I guess you could call it a high-rise. No elevator, but what the heck, we climb up the laces.

And don't you dare call me old. I may be tired, but dang it, don't call me old. Yep, I get tired but there's a lot of life left in me. Over the years I may have put on a few pounds, but my body and my fat have become really good friends.

Yeah, I have a lot of kids. I took in the three miller's kids when the mill burned down and he couldn't support them anymore. The shoemaker's four kids came to me when his wife died and he couldn't keep them anymore. And little Liza, I found her in a basket settin' on my porch one morning. None of them eight kids are mine, but I surely do love them youngins.

Now I may have a lot of kids, but don't you dare say I don't know what to do. I have plenty to do and I do it well. Let me tell you, there's no washing machine in that shoe, but I do fine doin' the laundry in the creek out back.

About transportation, we get around just fine with Charley, our horse, and a bench wagon. Once a week it's my turn to wagon pool the kids to school. And our vegetable garden out in the back forty provides us all the food we need plus some left over to haul to market. I make a mighty good livin' for all those kids.

As far as clothes go, I weave and I sew. Why the quality of my weavin' is the talk of the town. And I can whip up a pair of britches and a tunic shirt in a cotton-pickin' minute.

I have to admit that keeping all the kids in shoes is a challenge. The only thing those kids wear out faster than shoes is me.

OK, one night I was pretty tired and the kids got plain broth without any bread. So it was only one night. Give me a break! Nobody warned me that those kids got into the pantry and ate all the bread. I baked up a batch the next day, didn't I?

Now about the whipping. Of course I whipped them all soundly...at Uno. We had a fierce game of Uno going after supper and I won by a mile. And then I tucked them all into bed.

So, there you have the truth about me. Don't believe everything you read in the press.

Author's Bio

JEAN MOSBY makes her home on Florida's West Coast. At age 79 Jean answered a call for volunteers to start a Readers' Theater group in the retirement village where she and her husband reside. Within months they were both on stage having fun acting out their roles in comedy skits. It wasn't long before she began writing her own skits, which led to this book. She hopes you will enjoy acting out these skits as much as she enjoyed writing them.

PHOTO CREDIT TO
MAIDA ATKINS